T0300617

PLANTAS

PLANTAS

MODERN VEGAN RECIPES FOR TRADITIONAL MEXICAN COOKING

ALEXA SOTO

PHOTOGRAPHS BY ALEXA SOTO

LITTLE, BROWN AND COMPANY
NEW YORK / BOSTON / LONDON

Voracious / Little, Brown and Company
Hachette Book Group
1290 Avenue of the Americas, New York, NY 10104
voraciousbooks.com

First Edition: August 2024

Voracious is an imprint of Little, Brown and Company, a division of Hachette Book Group, Inc.
The Voracious name and logo are trademarks of Hachette Book Group, Inc.

The publisher is not responsible for websites (or their content) that are not owned by the publisher.

The Hachette Speakers Bureau provides a wide range of authors for speaking events. To find out more, go to hachettespeakersbureau.com or email hachettespeakers@hbgusa.com.

Little, Brown and Company books may be purchased in bulk for business, educational, or promotional use. For information, please contact your local bookseller or the Hachette Book Group Special Markets Department at special.markets@hbgusa.com.

Photographs by Alexa Soto except: p. 5 (family portrait) by Samantha Guerrero, p. 26 (Musica en Español) by Asha Bailey, p. 28 (Alexa in kitchen) by Lindsey Harris, and additional photographs by Chancy James Arnold

Illustrations © Shutterstock

Book design by Rita Sowins / Sowins Design

ISBN 9780316495103
LCCN 2023949236

10 9 8 7 6 5 4 3 2 1

MOHN

Printed in Germany

To my husband, Chancy James, the most
incredible life partner.
Thank you for being my number one support in
chasing all my hopes and dreams.

*A mi hijo lindo, Santino, todo es para ti...
para que sepas que puedes hacer cualquier cosa que
sueñes en tu vida.*

CONTENTS

ENTRADAS Y ANTOJITOS | STARTERS AND LITTLE CRAVINGS ...93

TACOS ... 133

MOLE ... 157

PLATILLOS FUERTES | MAIN DISHES ... 169

INTRODUCTION

Mexican cooking is rooted in plants. Corn, beans, rice, tomatoes, cacao, chiles, spices, fruit, herbs...all come from the earth. A bowl of frijoles de la olla with cilantro and onion offers instant comfort. Rice, cinnamon, and water create the delicious horchata drink. Corn, slaked lime, and water make the most precious gift the Mayans and Aztecs gave us, the tortilla. Nuts, seeds, cacao, tomatoes, and chiles are the building blocks of the Mexican version of a mother sauce, mole.

If we look at the beginnings of Mexican cooking, we must look to the Indigenous peoples. The culinary creations of the Mayans and Aztecs were heavily rooted in plants. Corn, chiles, squash, and tomatoes were some of the staples of indigenous cooking, and the pre-Columbian diet thrived on and celebrated the culinary and medicinal properties of plant-based food. The Spaniards later brought additional plant-based foods such as fruits, spices, and rice, and introduced animal proteins like pigs, sheep, cows, and chickens.

When you step foot in a Mexican market, plant foods routinely take up roughly 70 percent of its offerings—hundreds of varieties of whole spices, herbs, legumes, grains, chiles, fruits, and vegetables. Vendors selling an array of fresh fruit juices, dozens of maize-based dishes, and vegetable accompaniments bring the marketplace to life in vibrant color.

The foundation of Mexico's most beloved dishes is maize (maíz), or dried corn on the stalk, that goes through a nixtamalization process to create the base for corn tortillas, tamales, pozole, and so many more dishes, many of which you will find in this book. The indigenous cooking technique of nixtamalization brings out several nutritional benefits from this incredible crop, including increased bioavailability of iron, niacin, and calcium. During the three-thousand-year-old process, the dried maize kernels are soaked and then cooked in an alkaline solution—often based around woodfire ash or slaked lime (calcium hydroxide)—to soften them, then ground into masa, to be used either fresh or in the form of the flour known as masa harina.

Mexican culture and cuisine are heavily driven by Mother Earth's offerings, and while plenty of animal products are used today, it is a culinary culture that naturally lends itself to embracing a plant-based diet. Beyond that, it is a cuisine that prioritizes the use of local ingredients and minimizing waste, two values that go hand in hand with plant-based cooking. As such, as you make your way through this cookbook, I recommend leaning on your local farmers' market whenever possible, cooking in season, and exploring ways to repurpose any leftover ingredients, whether by combining unused tomatoes, onion, and cilantro into a simple salsa, or using up pantry staples and produce lying around to make a mole.

It is my hope that through this book, I will help my readers connect not only to the roots of Mexican cooking through a plant-based lens but also to the core beliefs of Mexican cooking that honor the bounty of nature and intentionality in feeding those you love, and it is my honor and privilege to do so.

My Roots

"La familia es lo mas importante en la vida" (family is the most important thing in life) is a belief my dad has always preached proudly and instilled in my family throughout my entire life. I was born in San Diego, California, just 15 minutes from the Mexican border. The community in which I was raised was rich in Mexican culture, traditions, and food. My Mexican heritage was represented in my home, in the homes of my grandparents and family members, and in my community.

I am the granddaughter of four Mexican grandparents who exhibited immense strength and fortitude, inspiring their children and grandchildren to create lives full of love, resilience, and pride.

My paternal grandfather Manlio was born in Michoacán, Mexico, and my paternal grandmother Eva was born in El Paso, Texas, but grew up in a very small town in Jalisco, Mexico. The two met in Cuernavaca, got married, and went on to raise my father and his five siblings in Mexico City. My father moved to the United States in his late teens. He worked hard to become fluent in English, complete his education, and support himself in this new country.

My maternal grandfather Alfonso was from Sonora, Mexico, and my maternal grandmother Esther was from Jalisco. They each moved to Tijuana in their late teens, where they met, got married, and started a family. After they had their first two children, my grandparents immigrated from Tijuana to San Diego. My grandparents worked to give my mother and her four siblings a conventional life in the US. They adjusted to some American traditions and customs, while still placing importance on fostering their Mexican roots through language, food, and traditions.

I am so proud to be Mexican American. And yet, being the first or second generation in the United States can make it hard to stay in touch with one's roots while also trying to belong in a new country. There's an expression in Spanish that goes "Ni de aquí, ni de allá": Not from here, not from there. Living in the US, I don't always connect with American culture, and I see vast differences in how I was raised and what values and traditions were instilled in me. In the same breath, when I spend time in Mexico, I often feel not Mexican enough. It can be confusing, and I have found that I have to work a little harder to feel like I belong in both cultures.

In my family of immigrants and first-generation relatives, I've witnessed a deep desire to bring everyone together often, to love each other through connection, through homemade meals passed down from generation to generation, and through quality time. No matter where in the world we are, our family is our home. And more often than not, the element that brings us together, the glue that binds us, is food.

Spanish was my first language. When I started school at the age of five, I had a strong accent when speaking English. My mother convinced my siblings and me that our dad couldn't speak English for a large part of our childhood, just so that we wouldn't lose our Spanish as kids. While ultimately untrue, it worked!

My mom is a resilient, intelligent woman who saw so much value and importance in raising children who are bilingual, even though it was more work. I will always be grateful to her, even for the thousands of times she corrected my Spanish grammar.

I owe so much to my parents and grandparents—for working so hard to give us a life full of love in the US while also nurturing our Mexican culture, so it can live on through this generation and for generations to come.

I met my husband, Chancy, when I was 17 years old. I remember learning that he was half Mexican and immediately feeling a sense of comfort in that answer, expecting similarities between our upbringings and families. As we grew closer and I met his family, I came to see, however, that his experience as a Mexican American was vastly different from mine. His mom is third-generation, and she was raised by loving parents who, in the 1960s, were unfortunately encouraged not to teach their children Spanish in order to fit into the culture of American schooling and be afforded equal opportunities. This experience of losing some of one's own culture in a desire to assimilate is not unique, and many immigrants have chosen to prioritize their adopted culture in an effort to minimize that feeling of ni de aquí, ni de allá. Personally, I'm grateful my parents chose to honor their Mexican heritage through language, food, and family, although they found their own ways to embrace their Mexican Americanness. And although Chancy may not have grown up as immersed in Mexican culture as I did, he was able to experience his culture through food like frijoles de la olla, fresh tortillas made by his mom, and many trips to the panadería (Mexican bakery) with his grandparents. Food, as it is for many, was the thing that kept the culture alive within his family across generations.

When I was growing up, my Mexican culture was all I knew. It came through in the value placed on family and traditions surrounding food, whether special celebrations like birthdays and baptisms or an ordinary Sunday morning brunch. Driving over to my grandparents' home for a meal meant more than just delicious food; it also meant the hours spent at the dining table conviviendo (spending time together). Stories being told, many rounds of antojitos (appetizers, or "little cravings"), platos fuertes (main courses), postres (dessert), cafecito (coffee), music, and maybe a little chisme (gossip) involved. Sobremesa—which means "over the table" and refers to the tradition of spending time together after a meal—is something my family has always been good at, and I value it deeply as it's something so rich in love and intention and unique to my culture.

I will always hold on tightly to my Mexican roots by honoring my culture through food, traditions, and family. There is a beauty in feeding my family foods full of the authentic flavors I grew up with, sharing recipes that have a long lineage, and acknowledging the importance of keeping our culture alive through recipes. Playing music while I cook, feeding my family foods that their ancestors made in their kitchens, and fostering closeness through togetherness and gatherings is what life is and will always be about. It is my honor to pay homage to my culture in this way and keep it alive as my grandparents—especially those no longer with us—would have wanted for my children and future generations to come.

Cooking Plants, Keeping My Culture

Growing up, I was a kid who watched the Food Network more than the Disney Channel. At the time, I thought the chefs I watched on TV were my role models; I wanted to grow up to be just like them. As an adult, I have reflected on what and who really inspires me daily in the kitchen, and it's undoubtedly the incredible home cooks that I get to call family. My mother, my father, my grandmothers, my aunts, and my mother-in-law are the people I appreciate daily for my forever-evolving love of cooking.

I have memories watching my Abuelita Eva cook over huge steel pots, feeding our large family of cousins, aunts, and uncles. I admired her effortlessness in the kitchen so much. She would cook with so much pride, joy, and pure love. As everyone sat and ate at my grandparents' large dining table, my abuelita would not sit to join but instead would stand around the table and simply watch, offering more tortillas and second servings. Her love language was feeding her family, and you could positively feel the love.

When I think of memories of my Grandma Esther, I think about the home she created. My heart flutters and my body feels warm and cozy at the memory of walking into my grandma's home. Her kitchen was the source of some of the most comforting foods I've ever had. Barbacoa every Christmas, pan dulce from a local Mexican bakery, flour tortillas with butter and sugar, and huge pots of pozole or sopita de verduras. My grandmother was full of love and warmth, and it shined throughout her home and in her cooking.

I've always loved food and was never picky, always willing to try something new at least once. But even more than just enjoying delicious food, I was fascinated by cooking at a very young age. It was something that called to me. I wanted to create something with my hands, heart, and soul. I wanted to effortlessly move around the kitchen as I had seen my grandmothers do. I wanted to cook for others, but I also always knew in my heart that I wanted to do more. I wanted to dedicate my life to cooking.

I always had a deep desire to be in the kitchen and nurture this natural passion I knew I had in me, but I had zero culinary education. While I was surrounded by a family of incredible cooks, there was a lot I still needed to learn. It wasn't until I was 19 years old that I really stepped into the kitchen and began to practice and learn the art of being a great home cook. At that time, an unhealthy relationship with my body image, made worse by invasive diet culture of the early 2000s, ended up furthering my journey into cooking even more. Crash diets and an unhealthy desire to fit unrealistic beauty standards led me to spend more and more time in the kitchen, obsessing over what I ate, but I eventually came to see food as a means to healing, which also coincided with turning to plants as a source of nutrition.

In this time, many phone calls were made to family members asking for recipes and hours were spent at my local farmers' markets. As I learned about different foods and ingredients, I found myself questioning where my food came from and what my role was as a cook and consumer. I felt pulled to be more intentional and mindful in how I would go about my cooking journey.

My paternal grandmother, Eva

Left: My father's parents, Eva and Manlio

My parents, Eduardo and Lillian, in 1988

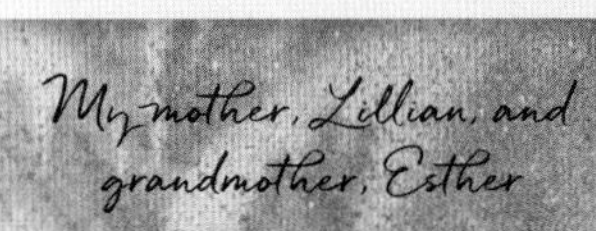

My mother, Lillian, and grandmother, Esther

My mother's parents, Alfonso and Esther

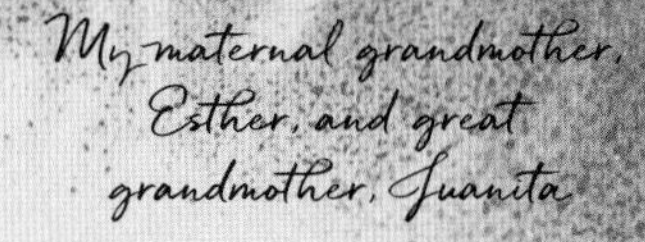

My maternal grandmother, Esther, and great grandmother, Juanita

In exploring new ways of thinking, I learned about the vegan diet, and I remember it was the first time I felt that I had come across a way of eating that had intention behind it. More than a diet, in fact, it was a lifestyle that challenged me to think about where my food was coming from and whether it was ethical and sustainable not just for my physical body but for the planet as well.

My parents were beyond shocked by the news that their food-loving, Food Network–obsessed daughter was going vegan. My dad's response was "Eso es lo que tu dices ahora…" (That's what you say now…), thinking it was a phase that would end in a week. My mother was mostly worried about what I was going to eat at family parties: "What are you going to tell your tías?" she asked, knowing that our traditions are always centered around food.

Within the first weeks of eating a vegan diet, I made another decision that changed my life forever. I started my blog, Fueled Naturally, and fell fully in love with cooking, plant-based eating, and sharing my life and recipes online. I was on a path toward what I had always dreamt of: a life spent dedicated to cooking.

Food is culture, and in Mexican culture, specific foods often bring everyone together. If it wasn't carne asada (a classic Mexican barbecue) on the weekends, it was spontaneous weekday nights spent at my grandparents' for my abuelita's tamales, chilaquiles on a weekend morning made by my tías, weeknight pozole at my grandma's, or celebrations like Día de Los Reyes, when a sweet bread called Rosca de Reyes was enjoyed.

Food brought us together, but so few of these dishes were vegan.

I wanted to live a life with morals that felt important to me, but I also wanted to stay true to my roots and hold onto my culture through food. So, I decided to do both. Traditional Mexican food is rooted in plants, so the transition felt natural in many ways. The more I traveled throughout Mexico and cooked old family recipes, the more inspiration I found in raw ingredients and their history. I began to see that there was an opportunity to highlight plants in my family's recipes, utilize indigenous cooking techniques, and include familiar Mexican ingredients but with an innovative plant-based approach. Over the past eight years I have found ways to veganize my most treasured family recipes and dishes.

Both of my grandmas have now passed on, and though they never cooked fully vegan meals, collecting their recipes has allowed me to feel their warm and loving presence around me. Through trial and error, learning and growing in the kitchen, I see my culture's food through a lens that goes all the way back to its roots: plants.

I hope that these recipes, so special to my family, can become special to you. Whether you are new to Mexican food, new to plant-based eating, or simply in love with flavor, I hope these recipes can serve as reasons to gather your favorite people together and enjoy a meal that nourishes both body and soul.

Buen provecho!

PLANTAS MEXICAN KITCHEN AND PANTRY

Traditional Mexican Kitchen Essentials

MOLCAJETE | MORTAR AND PESTLE

A traditional mortar and pestle made of volcanic rock, the molcajete was used by the Aztecs and Mayans to grind ingredients for things like moles, salsas, and guacamole.

In ditching the blender for a molcajete when making salsa, you get a deliciously rustic, chunky, almost jam-like texture that is truly unique—you can also use a regular mortar and pestle, but it won't quite achieve the consistency provided by the rough volcanic rock texture of the molcajete. There is also a "labor of love" element to preparing food with this special, ancient kitchen tool that makes the result feel that much more rewarding. It is important to cure a brand-new molcajete before using, as the volcanic rock is very porous. To avoid any grit in your salsas and guacamoles, a one-time cure is essential.

How to cure:

1. Put the molcajete in the sink. Add 2 tablespoons dish soap and a splash of water. Using a dish brush, vigorously scrub the entire inside and outside of the molcajete for 5 minutes, making sure to scrub every inch. Rinse the molcajete very well with water until the water runs mostly clear, then pour all the water out.
2. Add ¼ cup uncooked white rice and 1 tablespoon salt to the molcajete. Using the pestle, grind the rice until you reach a powder-like consistency. This will take 15 to 20 minutes.
3. Put the molcajete back in the sink, add a splash of water to the rice powder, and, using the pestle, spread the paste evenly, coating the entire inside of the molcajete.
4. Rinse the molcajete well with water until the water runs clear. Pour all the water out.
5. Add 3 peeled garlic cloves and, using the pestle, mash into a paste. Coat the entire inside of the molcajete with the garlic paste.
6. Return the molcajete to the sink one last time and rinse well with water. Your molcajete is cured and ready to use.

OLLA DE BARRO | CLAY POT

This traditional clay pot, which dates back over three thousand years, was used by Indigenous peoples to cook stews and beans and to make delicious Café de Olla (page 231), a traditional Mexican coffee. It is important to cure your olla de barro before use.

How to cure:

1. Rinse the olla de barro thoroughly with water.
2. Trim a sliver off the top of a peeled garlic clove and rub the cut garlic clove all over the outside of the olla de barro, to seal any cracks.
3. Fill the olla de barro with water until 2 inches from the top. Add ¼ cup baking soda and 1 cup white vinegar. Place on the stovetop, turn the heat to medium, and simmer for 4 hours, or until the liquid is reduced by half.
4. Remove from the heat and let cool for about 2 hours. Discard the liquid and wash the olla de barro with soap and water. Your olla de barro is ready to use.

TORTILLERO | TORTILLA HOLDER

A tortillero is essential when making homemade corn tortillas, as it allows them to steam. Even if you're using store-bought tortillas, a tortillero is great for keeping tortillas warm when serving family and friends. Heat a large batch of tortillas, store them in the tortillero, and place them in the center of the dining table for your guests to easily reach for a soft, warm tortilla. Woven or cloth tortilleros are my favorites.

PRENSA PARA TORTILLAS | TORTILLA PRESS

A tortilla press is a traditional kitchen device with two flat steel surfaces used to smash balls of masa (dough) into round corn tortillas, tetelas, and tlacoyos.

COMAL

A traditional pan dating back to 700 BCE, the comal is used for making tortillas, roasting chiles and vegetables for salsas, and preparing many antojitos using maize. Traditionally a comal was made of clay (barro), but today the comals used in most home kitchens are made of stainless steel, carbon steel, or cast iron. If you don't have a comal, a large skillet will work for these recipes.

BLENDER

A high-speed blender, like a Vitamix, is a dependable, time-saving kitchen tool to have, although the Oster One-Touch blender is also a great option at a quarter of the price. I have used both blenders to make every recipe in this book!

SAUTÉ PANS

I recommend having multiple sauté pans on hand to make these recipes, as you'll often need more than one at a time. My go-to is the 3.5-quart stainless-steel sauté pan from the brand Made In. I particularly love this pan for the rice dishes in this book, as a deep pan with a lid is essential for perfect Mexican rice.

Vegan Mexican Cooking and Pantry Essentials

FLOR DE JAMAICA | DRIED HIBISCUS FLOWERS

Dried hibiscus flowers originally came from Jamaica and are enjoyed in a Jamaican beverage called sorrel. The hibiscus flower was brought to Mexico during the American colonial period and is used in one of the most popular aguas frescas: Agua de Piña y Jamaica (page 228). Dried hibiscus flowers have numerous health properties, and studies have even shown it to be a natural antidepressant. Hibiscus flowers are also used in Chamoy (page 55), Taquitos de Flor de Jamaica (page 152), Conchas (page 210), and Ponche Navideño (page 249).

DRIED CHILES

When used in cooking, dried chiles add not only spice to a dish, but also sweet, smoky, and savory flavors that get overpowered by the spice when the chile is still fresh. Some of the most important dried chiles in Mexican cooking are chipotle, pasilla, chile de árbol, guajillo, and ancho.

NUTS AND SEEDS

Nuts and seeds are often used in traditional dishes like moles and salsas to bring a nutty, creamy, earthy element to a dish. This technique dates back to the Indigenous peoples of Mexico grinding pumpkin seeds into sauces using an ancient kitchen tool called a metate, which looks kind of like a flat pestle with a short rolling pin. Nuts and seeds to stock in your pantry include sesame seeds, pumpkin seeds, cashews, almonds, and peanuts. If I call for raw nuts, make sure they're unsalted.

YACA | JACKFRUIT

Jackfruit is a large, oval fruit native to Asia, Africa, and South America. The outside of a jackfruit is bumpy, rough, and green, with little pods of soft, springy, sweet fruit on the inside that taste similar to Juicy Fruit gum when ripe. Before the jackfruit ripens, however, the fruit pods are savory and pull apart similarly to cooked chicken or pulled pork, making for a great meat substitution. I recommend buying cans or pouches of young jackfruit in brine. You'll use jackfruit to make my Tamales Verdes (page 120), Taquitos de Yaca (page 136), Tacos de "Carnitas" (page 154), Birria (page 174), and Enchiladas Suizas (page 189).

CARNE DE SOYA | TEXTURED VEGETABLE PROTEIN (TVP)

Carne de soya may not be used every day by most Mexican families, but it is available at all Mexican grocery stores. You may also be able to find it, labeled TVP, at some specialty grocery stores. It is commonly used as a meat replacement in vegetarian and vegan restaurants across Mexico. This widely available and affordable dehydrated soy product is used in Hongos Portobello y Soya Asada Tacos (page 134) and Gringa al Pastor Tacos (page 141).

SETAS | OYSTER MUSHROOMS

Setas (oyster mushrooms) are truly Earth's gift. In Mexico, setas are widely available in markets, and in the US they have recently begun showing up as an additional option besides the common cremini or portobello mushroom. The texture is meaty and the flavor is savory yet subtle and takes on seasonings very well, similar to animal protein. When cooked with love and intention, oyster mushrooms make for a great meat substitution and can really shine as the main character in a dish. Look for setas in my Tacos de "Chicharrón" de Setas en Salsa Verde (page 149), Tacos de "Carnitas" (page 154), Mole Negro con Setas Asadas (page 159), and Birria (page 174).

NOPAL | PRICKLY PEAR CACTUS

Nopal is a cactus with leaves the shape of a paddle and large thorns that need to be removed before cooking. They have a unique texture and earthy, tart flavor. Nopales can be slimy during preparation, although depending on your preference you can remove that texture (following my instructions on page 102); either way it's a delightful vegetable with a satisfying bite and citrusy taste, not unlike okra. Nopales can often be found at a taquería as a vegetarian option or presented as a side for a touch of freshness. They are nutritious, too—rich in antioxidants, vitamins, and minerals. Nopal is the superfood of Mexican cuisine! Enjoy nopales in Guisado de Papas y Nopales en Salsa Roja Cremosa (page 71) or Ensalada de Nopales (page 102).

TOMATILLOS | MEXICAN HUSK TOMATOES

Tomatillos (meaning "little tomatoes") are a type of Mexican husk tomato, often much smaller than a classic tomato, with bitter, apple-like notes. Most of the time, tomatillos in the United States are a solid green color, averaging from the size of a cherry to the size of a small plum, with a papery husk. In Mexico, tomatillos often lean on the smaller side and are typically a combination of green and purple hues. You'll use tomatillos in many recipes in this book, such as Salsa Verde (page 81) and Pozole Verde (page 193).

PILONCILLO | CANE SUGAR CONE

Piloncillo is made by boiling and evaporating sugarcane juice, and it's often packaged in a cone shape. It's used to sweeten many drinks and dishes in Mexican cooking, especially Café de Olla (page 231). The flavor is rich, similar to the taste of brown sugar, with notes of caramel or even rum.

AVOCADO OIL

Avocado oil is the oil I reach for most in my kitchen for its neutral flavor and high smoke point. I like Chosen Foods brand. I especially love avocado oil for pan-frying vegetables such as mushrooms to reach a beautiful golden color and crisp texture.

> A note about pan-frying: Throughout my recipes, you'll see that I instruct you to pan-fry vegetables and other ingredients in batches. This is to ensure your ingredients all fry to a satisfying crispness. Please stick to these instructions, even if it might add a bit to your cook time—I promise it's worth it!

CHAMOY

This tangy, sweet, sometimes spicy condiment is made from dried fruit, chiles, and dried hibiscus flowers. Chamoy makes its way onto many street food indulgences, where it's drizzled on potato chips, ice cream, and even tropical fruits like mango. There are different types of chamoy, varying in consistency from a runny texture similar to Italian dressing to a thicker consistency similar to caramel. The runnier version is great drizzled on fruits and antojitos and the thicker version makes for the most satisfying cocktail rim. Mega and Amor brands can be found online or in Mexican grocery stores, or try my homemade Chamoy recipe (page 55).

TAJÍN SEASONING

Tajín is a Mexican seasoning with a granular consistency—like a dense salt—made of a blend of mild chiles, lime, and sea salt. You can find it in many supermarkets as well as in Mexican grocery stores and online. To add a punch of delicious flavor, sprinkle Tajín on Esquites (page 99) or fresh mango, or use to rim the beverage of your choosing.

POBLANO PEPPER

A mild chile that originated in the state of Puebla, the poblano pepper has a texture similar to bell pepper and is best prepared when roasted over an open flame until reaching charred perfection. Poblanos are widely available in US supermarkets, but note that they are often labeled as pasilla peppers. The poblano is *the* pepper in Mexican cuisine and is used in many recipes, such as Rajas y Papas en Crema Poblana (page 60) and Chiles Rellenos de Papa y Queso (page 184).

EPAZOTE

Epazote is a fragrant herb that is common in Mexican kitchens. It has notes of anise, mint, and licorice. A little goes a long way; only a couple leaves are needed in a big pot of Sopita de Lentejas (page 95) or in a batch of homemade Esquites (page 99). Epazote can be found fresh in Mexican grocery stores or dried online.

BLACK SALT

Black salt, also known as kala namak, is a popular ingredient in South Asian cuisines. Despite its name, this Himalayan black salt has a pinkish-brown color. It has a pungent smell, like an egg yolk, and for this very reason is perfect in dishes like Tofu a la Mexicana (page 58) to achieve a similar flavor profile to eggs.

MASA HARINA | NIXTAMALIZED CORN FLOUR

Masa harina translates to "dough flour" in English. It's not to be confused with typical corn flour or cornmeal, but instead is made from maize, which goes through the nixtamalization process: the dried corn from the stalk is boiled in an alkaline solution (limewater or, traditionally, woodfire ash mixed with water), then soaked overnight. Once softened, the outer layer is rubbed off each kernel before the maize is milled or ground into a dough. I use masa harina to make tortillas, tamales, tlacoyos, and other dishes. My favorite brands of masa harina (sometimes labeled instant corn masa flour) are Maseca and Masienda. You can find white, yellow, blue, and red masa harina, made from different maize varieties.

PLANT-BASED DAIRY SUBSTITUTES

Most grocery stores in the US carry a wide variety of plant-based products to use in place of dairy in these recipes. Try a few different brands to see what you like best; I prefer Miyoko's, Violife, Follow Your Heart, and Earth Balance for everything from shredded mozzarella-style cheese to vegan butter to sour cream. For plant-based milk, I get the best results in my recipes with almond, soy, or oat milk, and for condensed milk, I either make my own Lechera (page 203) or use a can of Nature's Charm vegan condensed milk.

MUSICA EN ESPAÑOL

Music is incredibly important to Mexican culture. In my parents' home, in my kitchen, in the homes of my relatives, in my everyday life, whether I am cooking or cleaning, music is always playing to grace my ears, mind, and soul with whatever it needs in the moment. Calmness, joy, or physical movement can all be inspired by Latin music. No matter how small the gathering, in my family it always includes music. A weekly Monday night dinner at my parents means salsa music is playing on the speakers throughout the home. A family party, no matter how casual or whatever the occasion, typically ends in a night of dancing and singing to reggaeton. Cleaning Sundays with my husband mean cumbias if he is in charge of music or every Selena song that exists if I am playing the tunes that day. I hope you'll let music whisk you away as you prepare these meals from my kitchen to yours!

LOS BÁSICOS

The Basics

✳ TORTILLAS DE HARINA ✳

Flour Tortillas

MAKES 8 TORTILLAS

1½ cups all-purpose flour, plus more for dusting

¾ teaspoon sea salt

¼ cup vegetable shortening

2 tablespoons neutral oil, such as avocado oil

½ cup warm water

My grandfather Alfonso believed any meal without a flour tortilla accompanying it was not complete. "No me sabe la comida cuando no hay tortilla de harina" (Food does not taste the same without flour tortillas)...which is a very Norteño (a person from northern Mexico) thing to say, as flour tortillas are eaten much more often than corn tortillas in the North. They're pure comfort, and once you've made them at home, there's no going back: you can't imagine eating another store-bought flour tortilla ever again. These tortillas are perfectly soft, buttery, and fluffy. I learned how to make them from my mother-in-law, Theresa, who learned from her Mexican mother and grandmother as a young girl. I adapted her recipe, swapping the lard for vegetable shortening and avocado oil, and she gave them a big stamp of approval! I think my grandfather would even have approved.

---

1. In a large bowl, mix the flour and salt, then add the shortening and oil. Using a fork, mix until you reach a wet sand texture.

2. Slowly add the warm water, a little at a time, mixing with your hands until a dough begins to form. Transfer to a work surface lightly dusted with flour and knead for 1 minute.

3. Divide the dough into 8 equal portions. Shape into balls, then cover with a kitchen towel or plastic wrap and let rest for 15 minutes. Heat a comal or large skillet over medium heat.

4. Lightly sprinkle about 1 tablespoon flour on a work surface. Grab a dough ball and stretch it into a 4-inch round with your hands. Place on the floured surface.

5. Using a lightly floured rolling pin, roll the circle of dough 2 to 5 times, then rotate the dough about 1 inch and roll another 2 or 3 times. Repeat rotating and rolling until you have an even, round tortilla, about ⅛ inch thick.

6. If you want to enjoy the tortillas right away, simply cook them one by one for 45 to 60 seconds on each side, until brown bubbles form.

7. If you are preparing the tortillas to be enjoyed later, my tip is to "half cook" them: Cook each tortilla for just 10 to 15 seconds on each side, then store in a ziplock bag in the fridge for up to a week. When ready to serve, reheat for 45 seconds to 1 minute in the comal over medium heat, until brown bubbles form.

TORTILLAS DE MAÍZ

Corn Tortillas

MAKES 8 TORTILLAS

1 cup masa harina (instant/nixtamalized corn masa flour)

Sea salt

¾ to 1 cup warm water

Squash blossoms (optional)

The foundation of all Mexican cuisine is the precious, very loved corn tortilla. These earthy, soft, thin handheld disks were a staple in Mayan and Aztec diets: the first corn tortillas are believed to have been made around 10,000 BCE, making this a truly ancient food. The corn tortilla does not begin with the ordinary corn we see in the United States but rather with maíz (maize). Maize is dried corn on the stalk that then goes through the nixtamalization process to create masa harina, which is then hydrated to make a dough.

The maize that is grown in Mexico comes in all shapes, colors, and sizes, leading to a variety of different colored tortillas and masa-based dishes, with the most typical being white, yellow, red, and blue. As an example of how resourceful and economical traditional Mexican cooking is, you need only three ingredients to make corn tortillas at home: masa harina, water, and salt. I often say that making corn tortillas requires less of an exact recipe and more of a feeling. There is a base recipe and key steps to consider in my recipe here, although the weather when you make the tortillas can determine if you need a little less or a little more water when making your dough. If you want to get creative, squash blossoms, hoja santa, or any edible flowers are a stunning way to transform your tortillas into art.

---

1. Combine the masa harina and a good pinch of salt in a large bowl. Add ¾ cup warm water and mix with your hands to form a dough. Transfer to a work surface and knead for 5 minutes.

2. Wash and dry your hands, then take a golf ball–size piece of dough and roll it into a smooth ball between your palms. Use your thumb to press into the center of the ball. The dough should not stick to your thumb and the edges should not crack: if the edges show cracks, slowly add the remaining ¼ cup warm water and continue to bring the mixture together. Knead for another 5 minutes. Form the remaining dough in the same way, then return the dough balls to the bowl. Cover the bowl with plastic wrap and let the dough rest for 10 minutes.

3. Meanwhile, if you're using squash blossoms, cut off the bottoms and remove the inside bulbs.

4. Cut open a large ziplock bag or plastic produce bag, lay one piece across the bottom of your tortilla press, and set aside the other piece to lay over the dough. (Alternatively, you can use plastic wrap or parchment paper.)

5. Heat a comal or large skillet over medium heat.

6. Place one masa ball on the plastic-covered base of the tortilla press. Cover the dough with the other piece of plastic and gently lower the press to flatten the dough ball to about ¼ inch thick, then open it up.

7. Remove the top piece of plastic and add a squash blossom, if using, to the center of the dough circle. Cover with the plastic again, rotate the tortilla 180 degrees, then press the dough again to about ⅛ inch thick. If you're not adding squash blossom, simply rotate 180 degrees and press again.

8. Open the press and gently peel the tortilla off the plastic. It should come off in one piece; if it rips, press more gently on the next tortilla.

9. Place the tortilla in the hot pan and cook for about 20 seconds on one side, then flip and cook for an additional 50 to 60 seconds. Flip once more and cook for 10 seconds, or until air bubbles form. You can press the center of the tortilla with your hands or a spatula to encourage it to puff up. Transfer the cooked tortilla to a tortilla holder or wrap in a kitchen towel. Repeat with the remaining dough balls. Let the tortillas rest for 1 to 2 minutes before serving.

MAYONESA DE LIMÓN

Mexican Lime Mayonnaise

MAKES 1½ CUPS

What makes Mexican mayonnaise different from—and, in my opinion, better than—the standard American mayonnaise is its subtle lime flavor. Homemade vegan mayonnaise is so simple to make and is creamier, smoother, more delicious, and healthier than the store-bought kind. I find that soy milk works best in making a creamy, thick mayonnaise thanks to its high protein content, although you can use most plain, unsweetened nondairy milks (they just may yield runnier results). Mexican mayo is a must-add to Esquites (page 99), Ceviche de Palmito (page 109), or my Quesadillas de "Atún" de Garbanzo (page 105).

½ cup plain, unsweetened soy milk

2 tablespoons fresh lime juice

¾ teaspoon sea salt

1 cup neutral oil, such as avocado oil

1. Combine the milk, lime juice, and salt in a tall jar. Using a handheld blender, begin to pulse the mixture, slowly adding the oil and moving the blender up and down until all the oil has been added and the mayo becomes thick and creamy. (This will yield a thick mayo; if you're not as concerned about the consistency or are short on time, you can combine all the ingredients at once and blend with a handheld blender or in a countertop blender for about 20 seconds.)
2. Use right away or store in a covered container in the fridge for up to 2 weeks.

CREMA MEXICANA

Mexican Sour Cream

MAKES 1½ CUPS

Crema Mexicana was an absolute staple in our fridge growing up. Similar to sour cream but thinner and slightly sweeter, it's perfect for drizzling over enchiladas, chilaquiles, and even Arroz Rojo (page 44). I make my plant-based version with cashews, which makes for a dreamy, creamy consistency without adding too much nutty flavor. If you prefer a spicy sauce, add the optional chipotle chiles.

---

1 cup raw cashews

1 cup plain, unsweetened plant-based milk

2 tablespoons fresh lime juice

1 teaspoon onion powder

½ teaspoon garlic powder

½ teaspoon sea salt

3 or 4 canned chipotle chiles in adobo (optional)

1. Put the cashews in a bowl, cover with boiling water, and let soak for 15 minutes. (Alternatively, you can soak the cashews overnight in room-temperature water.)

2. Drain the cashews and transfer to a blender. Add the milk, lime juice, onion and garlic powders, salt, and chipotles (if using) and blend on high for 1 minute. The mixture should be smooth and slightly runny so you can drizzle it easily; if necessary, add 1 to 2 tablespoons more milk. Taste the crema and add more salt to your liking.

3. Use right away or store in a covered container in the fridge for up to 6 days. The crema will get slightly thicker after refrigeration. To thin it out again, simply mix in another 1 to 2 tablespoons milk before serving.

❋ QUESO COTIJA Y LECHE DE ALMENDRA ❋

Mexican Crumbled Cheese and Almond Milk

MAKES 6 OUNCES CHEESE AND 2 CUPS MILK

1 cup raw almonds

2 cups water

½ teaspoon fresh lemon juice

⅛ teaspoon apple cider vinegar

½ teaspoon sea salt

Cotija is a staple in any Mexican fridge. It's an aged cheese usually made from cow's milk, and named after the city in Michoacán where it originated. I have dreamt of a vegan version for a long time, and I'm so happy to say this is *it*: a plant-based, salty, crumbly cheese ideal for topping enchiladas, tacos, Tostadas de Champiñones (page 170), or even a bowl of Frijoles de la Olla (page 48). As often happens with the best recipes, this one magically happened by chance. One day, I was making homemade almond milk and instead of throwing out the leftover almond pulp, I noticed it had exactly the texture of Cotija cheese. I started with this inspiration and immediately got to work. The result is a vegan two-for-one: you get plant cheese *and* plant milk out of this recipe! The creamy, delicious almond milk is perfect for a recipe like Calabaza en Tacha (page 207) or a latte. *Note: You will need a nut milk bag or cheesecloth to make this recipe.*

---

1. Put the almonds in a bowl, cover with boiling water, and let soak for 15 minutes.

2. After 15 minutes, use a spoon to fish out one almond and remove the skin by squeezing the almond between your thumb and index finger. The skin should pop right off. If it does not, the almonds need to soak for a little longer. If the almonds are ready, drain the almonds and remove the skins.

3. Transfer the almonds to a blender, add the water, and blend on high for 1 minute.

4. Place a nut milk bag or cheesecloth over a large bowl and pour the blended mixture through it into the bowl. Gently squeeze the bag or cloth with both hands and let the almond milk drip into the bowl. Set aside the bag of almond pulp. The almond milk might be thicker than you're used to at this point, but you can add 1 to 2 cups additional water for a thinner consistency. I recommend adding a pinch of salt to the milk. Transfer to a covered container and store in the fridge for up to 5 days.

5. Open the nut milk bag and dump the pulp into a bowl. Add the lemon juice, vinegar, and salt and use your hands to form the mixture into a ball. Wrap in plastic wrap and refrigerate overnight. When ready to use, break off as much as you want and crumble with your fingers. It will keep in the fridge for up to 6 days.

JALAPEÑOS Y ZANAHORIAS EN ESCABECHE

Quick-Pickled Jalapeños and Carrots

When I was growing up, my family always had a plastic container filled with pickled jalapeños and carrots in the fridge. Pickled veggies are a perhaps unknown staple in Mexican cooking, as they balance out some of the richer foods so well. You'll always find them served with carne asada, or available for topping tacos. While you can certainly find these canned in a grocery store, they're just too easy not to make at home, and can be a great way to use up vegetables lying around in the fridge. This recipe will make pickled veggies that pack a crisp, spicy, vinegary punch that is unmatched. They are especially great for pairing with a rich dish like Hongos Portobello y Soya Asada Tacos (page 134) or Sopes (page 96), as they cut through that richness and provide a balanced freshness, but they can also be enjoyed on their own, straight from the jar. They're *that* good.

MAKES 1 QUART

1½ cups water

1½ cups white wine vinegar

⅓ cup sugar

1½ tablespoons dried oregano

½ teaspoon sea salt

½ large white or red onion, thinly sliced

3 large carrots, peeled and sliced into thin rounds

4 jalapeño peppers, cut into ¼-inch-thick slices

---

1. In a medium pot, combine the water, vinegar, sugar, oregano, and salt. Bring to a simmer, then turn off the heat and allow to cool for 10 minutes.

2. Put the onion, carrots, and jalapeños in a quart-size jar, then pour the liquid over the vegetables. Let the vegetables sit at room temperature, uncovered, for 1 hour.

3. The pickled vegetables are now ready to enjoy, or cover and refrigerate overnight for a stronger pickled flavor and even better texture. Store in the fridge for up to 3 weeks.

ABUELITA'S ARROZ BLANCO

Grandma's Mexican White Rice

SERVES 4 OR 5

1 poblano pepper (sometimes labeled pasilla pepper)

1 cup long-grain white rice

2 tablespoons neutral oil, such as avocado oil

¼ small white onion, finely diced

1 large garlic clove, minced

1 large carrot, peeled and finely diced

1 ear corn, kernels cut off the cob

1¾ cups low-sodium vegetable broth

1 lime, halved

½ teaspoon sea salt

1 cilantro sprig

My Abuelita Eva would make a vegetable-laden white rice religiously, and it's become such a nostalgic dish for me. Five years ago, I began to make rice from a version of the recipe that was passed down through my abuelita, then to my Tía Cristy, then to my mom, but I found it just didn't taste exactly like my abuelita's. Wanting to recreate that nostalgic dish, I asked my tía for my abuelita's rice secrets. She shared that the key is to ditch the bag of frozen vegetables that most Mexican families use in their rice, and follow my abuelita's lead by using only fresh vegetables.

There was something so incredibly special about my abuelita's cooking, and I think it is due to the intentionality and time she dedicated to cooking. Nowadays, it seems that there is a big dependence on convenience and finding the fastest way to put a meal on the table, but for my abuelita, being born in the 1920s—before fast food, frozen dinners, or prepared meals—meant an abundance of fresh ingredients were the norm, making her food creations that much more delicious, grounding, and wholesome. No matter how times evolved around her, she stuck to her principles in the kitchen, where the importance of fresh ingredients remained cherished above all in her recipes. You can of course make great rice with a bag of mixed frozen vegetables, but going back to the roots and following my abuelita's lead with fresh veggies makes all the difference. This rice pairs perfectly with Mole Verde con Tofu (page 162) or Mole Negro con Setas Asadas (page 159).

---

1. Roast the poblano pepper on an open flame for 1 to 2 minutes, until charred on all sides. (Alternatively, heat the oven to the highest broiler setting, put the poblano pepper on a rimmed baking sheet lined with aluminum foil, and broil on the middle oven rack for 1 to 2 minutes on each side, until charred.) Transfer the poblano pepper to a bowl, cover with plastic wrap, and let sit for 10 minutes to release steam.

2. While the poblano pepper is steaming, put the rice in a fine-mesh strainer and rinse well under cool running water. Set the strainer over a large bowl or suspended in the sink to allow the rice to continue to drain while you cook the vegetables.

(Continued)

(Continued)

3. Heat the oil in a large sauté pan over medium-low heat. Add the onion and sauté for 1 minute. Add the garlic, carrot, and corn kernels, turn the heat down to low, and cook for 3 to 4 minutes.

4. Remove the charred skin, stem, inner ribs, and seeds from the poblano pepper. Slice into thin 1-inch-long strips. Add the poblano pepper to the vegetable mixture in the pan and cook for 3 minutes.

5. Add the rice to the pan, turn the heat up to medium-high, and stir continuously for 2 minutes. Do not stop stirring!

6. Add the broth, juice of one lime half, and salt and bring to a simmer. Stir, cover, turn the heat down to low, and cook for 19 to 22 minutes, until the liquid has been absorbed and the rice is fluffy.

7. Remove the pan from the heat and let the rice sit, covered, for 10 minutes. Garnish with the cilantro and squeeze over the juice from the remaining lime half.

ARROZ ROJO

Mexican Red Rice

SERVES 4 OR 5

1 cup long-grain white rice

½ medium white onion, ¼ roughly chopped and ¼ finely diced

2 garlic cloves, peeled, 1 left whole and 1 minced

2 ripe Roma tomatoes, halved

2 cups low-sodium vegetable broth, divided

2 tablespoons neutral high-heat oil, such as avocado oil

½ teaspoon sea salt

3 cilantro sprigs

1 serrano pepper, slit lengthwise (optional)

Making a good red rice is one of the most important lessons of Mexican cooking, but it can also feel like the most intimidating because of all the steps required. When I moved out of my parents' home, there were many things I knew I needed to learn how to make from my mom, and this was at the top of the list. Some tips for success: First, you'll need a deep sauté pan or skillet with a lid, as a regular pot will not yield the same results. Second, being very present when you first start cooking the rice is key to ensuring it achieves a perfect golden color. And third, opting to make a fresh, easy tomato sauce (rather than the canned or jarred stuff) is so worth it! This rice is a classic that pairs nicely with any taco recipe or serves as a great side for your next family gathering.

---

1. Put the rice in a fine-mesh strainer and rinse well under cool running water. Set the strainer over a large bowl or suspended in the sink to allow the rice to continue to drain while you prepare the salsa.

2. In a blender, combine the roughly chopped onion, whole garlic clove, tomatoes, and ½ cup broth. Blend on high for 1 minute, or until relatively smooth.

3. Heat the oil in a large, deep sauté pan over medium-high heat. Add the rice, turn the heat up to high, and cook, stirring continuously, for 2 minutes, or until the rice is golden. Do not stop stirring!

4. Turn the heat down to low, add the diced onion and minced garlic, and sauté for 1 minute, or until the onion is translucent.

5. Add about half of the blended tomato salsa to the pan, stir to combine, and cook for 2 minutes. Add the rest of the salsa and cook for 3 minutes, stirring frequently, until the rice absorbs most of the liquid.

6. Add the remaining 1½ cups broth and the salt, stir, and bring to a simmer. Add 2 cilantro sprigs and the serrano pepper. Cover, turn the heat down to low, and cook for 19 to 22 minutes, until the liquid has been absorbed and the rice is fluffy.

7. Remove the pan from the heat and let the rice sit, covered, for 10 minutes. Garnish with the remaining cilantro sprig. If you like, you can quickly pan-fry the serrano pepper to get some nice char on it and place it on top.

ARROZ VERDE

Mexican Green Rice

SERVES 4 OR 5

1 cup long-grain white rice

½ white onion, ¼ roughly chopped and ¼ finely diced

2 garlic cloves, peeled, 1 left whole and 1 minced

5 tomatillos, husked

2 jalapeño peppers, 1 stemmed and seeded and 1 quartered lengthwise

½ cup baby spinach

½ bunch cilantro

2 cups low-sodium vegetable broth, divided

3 tablespoons neutral high-heat oil, such as avocado oil, divided

½ teaspoon sea salt

A beautiful Mexican rice with an extra layer of sazón, arroz verde is a savory, flavorful side dish you don't see as often as white or red rice in Mexican homes. But each time I make it, I wonder why it isn't more of a staple in everyone's kitchens and at every gathering—it's that good! Because this rice does not have traditional roots but rather is a play on Arroz Rojo (page 44), there's more room for creativity. I love the addition of spinach for the added nutrients and the deep green hue it creates, but you can play around with additional ingredients to give the rice its beautiful color. The combination of tomatillos, jalapeños, and cilantro makes for an herbaceous, tart, slightly spicy sauce that gets absorbed right into the toasted rice. Herby and fluffy, this rice dish pairs beautifully with Enchiladas Suizas (page 189) or Tacos de "Carnitas" (page 154).

---

1. Put the rice in a fine-mesh strainer and rinse well under cool running water. Set the strainer over a large bowl or suspended in the sink to allow the rice to continue to drain while you prepare the salsa.
2. In a blender, combine the roughly chopped onion, whole garlic clove, tomatillos, stemmed and seeded jalapeño, spinach, cilantro and ½ cup broth. Blend on high for 1 minute, or until relatively smooth.
3. Heat 2 tablespoons oil in a large, deep sauté pan over medium-high heat. Add the rice, turn the heat up to high, and cook, stirring continuously, for 2 minutes, or until the rice is golden. Do not stop stirring!
4. Turn the heat down to low, add the diced onion and minced garlic, and sauté for 1 minute, or until the onion is translucent.
5. Add about half of the blended green salsa to the pan, stir to combine, and cook for 2 minutes. Add the rest of the salsa and cook for 3 minutes, stirring frequently, until the rice absorbs most of the liquid.
6. Add the remaining 1½ cups broth and the salt and bring to a simmer. Cover, reduce the heat to low, and cook for 19 to 22 minutes, until the liquid has been absorbed and the rice is fluffy.
7. Remove the pan from the heat and let the rice sit, covered, for 10 minutes. While the rice is sitting, heat the remaining 1 tablespoon oil in a small skillet over medium heat. Add the quartered jalapeño and pan-fry for 1 to 2 minutes, until charred on both sides. Garnish the rice with the charred jalapeño.

FRIJOLES DE LA OLLA

Stovetop Beans

SERVES 7 OR 8

2 cups dried pinto, black, or Peruvian beans

About 10 cups water

1 medium white onion, halved

6 garlic cloves, peeled

2 bay leaves

1 jalapeño or serrano pepper, slit lengthwise

3 tablespoons olive oil

1 teaspoon sea salt

Chopped fresh cilantro, for garnish

Queso Cotija (page 38) or store-bought vegan feta, for garnish

Corn or flour tortillas, store-bought or homemade (pages 34 and 30), warmed, for serving

When I was a kid, my favorite food to come home to after school was a bowl of frijoles de la olla (beans from the pot), topped with cilantro and onion and sometimes cheese, and accompanied by a side of warm tortillas. I remember walking into my home and instantly getting a cozy feeling from the smell of the beans my mom had gently simmering on the stove. Preparing a pot of beans is an essential element of Mexican life, as important as drinking water and getting sleep: beans can always be found as a side dish or even a meal in and of themself. For me, preparing a pot of beans is a weekly ritual, an opportunity to slow down and be present and aware of each little bean I sort through.

---

1. Put some music on (see page 27), light a candle (yes, both essential parts of this recipe!), and sort through the beans, removing any pebbles. There won't be a ton, but you may find 1 or 2 in each bag of beans. Put the beans in a fine-mesh strainer and rinse under cool running water. Drain well.

2. Transfer the beans to a large pot, Dutch oven, or cured olla de barro (see page 20) and pour in enough water to cover the beans by about 4 inches. Add the onion halves, garlic cloves, and bay leaves. Cook the beans over medium-low heat for about 2½ hours, without covering or stirring, until tender. Throughout the cooking process, the beans should be at a soft boil—adjust the heat accordingly. The water will evaporate, so you will need to add 1 cup hot water every 30 minutes.

3. Once the beans are done (you can check the doneness by mashing a single cooked bean with the back of a wooden spoon or spatula: it should mash like softened butter), add the jalapeño or serrano pepper, olive oil, and salt. Stir, then reduce the heat to low and simmer for 30 more minutes. The liquid in the pot, now a bean broth, should be reduced and slightly thickened. Taste the beans and broth and add more salt if needed.

4. Before serving, remove the bay leaves. (You can also remove the garlic and onion, but I like to leave them in.) Serve the beans hot with a few ladles of broth, topped with chopped cilantro and crumbled Cotija, and with a side of warm tortillas.

FRIJOLES REFRITOS

Refried Beans

SERVES 5 OR 6

3 tablespoons neutral oil, such as avocado oil

¼ medium white onion, diced small

1 jalapeño pepper, seeded and diced small

3 garlic cloves, minced

4 cups cooked or canned pinto, black, or Peruvian beans

¼ to ½ cup bean broth from homemade beans or low-sodium vegetable broth, divided

½ teaspoon sea salt

Queso Cotija (page 38) or storebought vegan feta, for garnish

Cooked beans gently pan-fried in a little oil with spice, onion, and garlic and then mashed until creamy is the ultimate comfort dish in Mexican homes. There was nothing I loved more than when my mom would throw refried beans in a fluffy flour tortilla to make bean burritos for me to take to school. It looked different from the average school lunch, considering most students enjoyed their classic American sandwiches, but I preferred my warm little burrito 100 times over.

There are several brands of canned refried beans in grocery stores across the US, but none will even come close to the authenticity and flavor you can easily create in your kitchen. If you don't have cooked-from-scratch beans on hand (see page 48) but have a can of pinto or black beans, they can also be a great start to making homemade refried beans! If you take the time to make refried beans, I strongly suggest you also make a batch of homemade Tortillas de Harina (page 30) for your own happy little warm bean-burrito bundles. Refried beans can also be served as a side, or used in recipes such as Tostadas de Champiñones (page 170) or Sopes (page 96).

---

1. Heat the oil in a large sauté pan over low heat. Add the onion and sauté for 2 minutes, then add the jalapeño and garlic and sauté for 2 minutes. Turn the heat up to medium, add the beans and ¼ cup broth, and simmer for 3 minutes.

2. Turn the heat down to low and, using a potato masher or the back of a fork, mash the beans until you reach the desired consistency. Add the salt and stir. If the beans seem dry, stir in another ¼ cup broth. For extra smooth beans, you can carefully transfer everything to a blender and blend on high for 1 minute, or until smooth. Taste the beans and add more salt to your liking, and sprinkle with Cotija cheese, if desired.

BOLILLOS

Mexican Rolls

MAKES 6 ROLLS

1¼ cups plain, unsweetened plant-based milk

2 tablespoons cane sugar

2¼ teaspoons active dry yeast

3 cups all-purpose flour, divided, plus more for dusting

1 teaspoon sea salt

4 tablespoons olive oil or a neutral oil, such as avocado oil, divided, plus more for brushing

I can't step foot into a Mexican grocery store without running over to the bakery and checking to see if there are any freshly made bolillos. The moment my husband and I get in our car, we split one. We always have smiles on our faces as we joyfully devour the bread, which is gone in seconds. It is *the* bread roll of Mexican cuisine—a classic, similar to a French baguette, with a crusty, crunchy outside and a soft inside. Learning to make this Mexican staple is so worth it, requiring only a few simple ingredients and a nice relaxing hour of your time!

Bolillos are often used to make tortas (Mexican sandwiches) and a popular Mexican breakfast called molletes—for the latter, simply cut a warm bolillo in half lengthwise, then spread on a generous layer of Frijoles Refritos (page 51) and top with sliced avocado and crumbled Queso Cotija (page 38). Bolillos can also be torn into pieces to scoop up the salsa from chilaquiles, Chilango-style (as a person from Mexico City would do). My godmother, Maru, is a Chilanga through and through and *always* serves bolillos with chilaquiles.

---

1. In a small heatproof bowl, microwave the milk for 1 minute, until warm to the touch but not hot. (Alternatively, heat the milk in a small saucepan over low heat.)

2. In a large bowl, combine the warm milk, sugar, and yeast and stir. Let sit for 10 minutes to activate the yeast; it should become frothy.

3. Add 2 cups flour and the salt and mix with a wooden spoon until just incorporated. Add 2 tablespoons oil and the remaining 1 cup flour. Mix again until the flour is incorporated.

4. Form the dough into a loose ball and transfer to a work surface generously dusted with flour. Knead with a firm hand for 6 to 8 minutes, until smooth. Pour the remaining 2 tablespoons oil into a clean bowl and use a paper towel to coat the inside of the bowl, then add the dough. Cover with plastic wrap or a kitchen towel and let rise for 1 hour in a warm, dark place; it should double in size.

5. Turn out the dough onto a lightly floured surface and divide into 6 equal portions. Use both hands to roll each portion into a ball, then press gently onto the countertop to flatten the bottom, keeping the top round and smooth. Transfer to a rimmed baking sheet and let sit for 10 minutes.

6. Use both hands to gently pull the ends and flatten the sides into an oval shape, similar to a baguette, then use a rolling pin to roll the oval until it is about 2 inches thick. Cover the ovals with plastic wrap and let rise for 30 minutes. They should double in size. Meanwhile, preheat the oven to 375°F.

7. Using a sharp knife, cut a slash straight down the middle of each oval, then brush the tops with oil. Let them sit, uncovered, for 10 minutes.

8. Bake for 20 to 25 minutes, until golden. Enjoy right away or store in a covered container at room temperature for up to 4 days.

CHAMOY

Hibiscus-Chile Sauce

MAKES 2 CUPS

- 1 cup dried hibiscus flowers
- ½ cup pitted prunes
- ½ cup pitted dried apricots
- 5 chiles de árbol, stemmed and seeded
- 5 cups water
- 2 cups cane sugar
- ½ cup fresh lime juice (from about 4 limes)
- ¼ cup Tajín Seasoning
- 2 teaspoons citric acid

A tangy, spicy, sweet sauce made of fruit, chiles, and dried hibiscus flowers, chamoy is never missing from the rims of my dad's margaritas, and once you make your own, it will never be missing from yours, either. This thick chamoy is equally tasty drizzled over fresh fruit like watermelon, cucumber, jicama, and mango. Hibiscus flowers, also known as flor de jamaica, can be found in the international aisle of the supermarket, and citric acid in the baking aisle, or online.

---

1. In a large pot, combine the hibiscus flowers, prunes, apricots, chiles, and water. Bring to a simmer over medium heat and simmer for 30 minutes.
2. Add the sugar, stir, and cook for 10 minutes, then remove the pot from the heat and let cool for 1 hour.
3. Transfer the cooled mixture to a blender or food processor, add the lime juice, Tajín, and citric acid, and blend until smooth. If the mixture is too thick and your blender is having a hard time, slowly add a couple tablespoons warm water. The consistency should be thick but smooth.
4. Use right away or store in a covered container in the fridge for up to 2 months.

DESAYUNOS

Breakfasts

❋ TOFU A LA MEXICANA ❋

Mexican Tofu Scramble

SERVES 6

1 (14- to 16-ounce) package firm or medium-firm tofu

½ teaspoon ground turmeric

½ teaspoon ground paprika

¼ to ½ teaspoon sea salt

¼ teaspoon black salt (kala namak; optional)

¼ teaspoon ground black pepper

1 tablespoon neutral oil, such as avocado oil

½ medium red onion, diced small

2 garlic cloves, minced

3 ripe Roma tomatoes, seeded and diced small

1 serrano or jalapeño pepper, seeded if desired and diced small

3 tablespoons Salsa Verde (page 81) or Salsa Asada (page 80)

3 tablespoons nutritional yeast (optional)

TO SERVE:

¼ bunch cilantro, chopped

1 avocado, halved, pitted, peeled, and sliced

Jalapeños y Zanahorias en Escabeche (page 40)

Salsa Asada (page 80)

Corn or flour tortillas, store-bought or homemade (pages 34 and 30), warmed

To say that something is "a la Mexicana" means it is prepared "Mexican-style," which typically means that the dish has tomato, serrano pepper, and onion, all core ingredients in Mexican cooking—also, fittingly, representing the red, green, and white colors of the Mexican flag.

When I moved out of my parents' home at 23 years old, one thing I knew I would miss deeply were mornings with my dad. We both are morning people, so it would often just be us two in the kitchen. We sipped on coffee, and he prepared breakfast as we shared the latest chisme (gossip). One of those typical weekday breakfasts was his huevos a la Mexicana, always prepared with lots of intention and love.

I was never able to fill the void left by losing those mornings with my dad, but I did set out to fill the void of his huevos a la Mexicana. Tofu makes an exceptional substitute for scrambled eggs, and when prepared "a la Mexicana," it transforms into the most flavorful scramble I've ever had. The addition of black salt (also known as kala namak) is optional but highly recommended to add an egglike flavor. Only the slightest bit is needed as it has a powerful taste and smell.

---

1. Wrap the tofu in a kitchen towel or paper towel and squeeze for 10 to 15 seconds to remove the excess water. Put the tofu in a large bowl and crumble it into small pieces. Add the turmeric, paprika, salt(s)—if using black salt, use only ¼ teaspoon sea salt—and pepper and mix with your hands, ensuring that the tofu pieces are well coated with the spices.

2. Heat the oil in a large nonstick skillet over medium-low heat. Add the onion and sauté for 2 minutes. Add the garlic and sauté for 1 minute. Add the tomatoes and serrano or jalapeño, stir, and cook for 3 minutes. Add the tofu and cook for 10 minutes, stirring frequently. Add the salsa and stir to combine.

3. Remove the pan from the heat, sprinkle the nutritional yeast (if using) over the tofu scramble, and give it another good mix. Taste and add more sea salt or black salt if needed.

4. Transfer the tofu scramble to a serving dish. Top with chopped cilantro, sliced avocado, pickled veg, and salsa. Serve with tortillas.

RAJAS Y PAPAS EN CREMA POBLANA

Creamy Roasted Poblano Pepper and Potato Hash

SERVES 5 OR 6

½ cup raw cashews

1 pound Yukon Gold potatoes, scrubbed and diced small

½ teaspoon plus a pinch sea salt

4 poblano peppers (sometimes labeled pasilla peppers)

2 tablespoons neutral oil, such as avocado oil

1 medium white onion, thinly sliced

3 garlic cloves, minced

½ bunch cilantro

1 cup low-sodium vegetable broth

¼ teaspoon ground black pepper

Corn or flour tortillas, store-bought or homemade (pages 34 and 30), warmed, for serving

One particular morning, during a long-term stay in CDMX (shorthand for Mexico City), I was standing in my best friend Sofia's kitchen, feeling inspired by this beautiful, bustling city. I put myself in charge of making breakfast and found myself reaching for produce and ingredients in her fridge that were begging to be cooked. Out came this divine breakfast hash, packed with flavor, spice, creaminess, and comfort. This dish makes a fantastic breakfast side or, thrown into a flour tortilla, delicious burritos.

---

1. Put the cashews in a bowl, cover with boiling water, and let soak for 15 minutes. (Alternatively, soak overnight in room-temperature water.)

2. While the cashews are soaking, put the potatoes in a medium pot, cover with water, and add a generous pinch of salt. Bring to a boil over high heat and boil for 15 to 17 minutes, until the potatoes are fork-tender. Drain.

3. While the potatoes are cooking, roast the poblano peppers on an open flame for 1 to 2 minutes, until charred on all sides. (Alternatively, heat the oven to the highest broiler setting, put the poblanos on a rimmed baking sheet lined with aluminum foil, and broil on the middle oven rack for 1 to 2 minutes on each side, until charred.) Transfer the poblano peppers to a bowl, cover with plastic wrap, and let sit for 10 minutes to release steam.

4. Heat the oil in a large skillet over medium-low heat. Add the onion and sauté for 6 to 8 minutes, until golden.

5. Remove the charred skin, stems, inner ribs, and seeds from the poblano peppers. Cut 3 of the poblano peppers into thin, 1-inch-long strips; leave the remaining poblano as is.

6. Transfer half of the sautéed onion to a blender. Turn the heat under the pan down to low, add the garlic, and sauté for 2 minutes.

7. Drain the soaked cashews and transfer to the blender with the onion. Add the whole poblano pepper, half of the cilantro, the broth, and the remaining ½ teaspoon salt and blend on high for 1 minute, or until smooth.

8. Pour the sauce over the onion and garlic in the pan, then add the poblano pepper strips and potatoes. Mix to combine.

9. Chop the remaining cilantro and add to the pan, mixing again. Add the black pepper, then taste and add more salt to your liking. Serve with tortillas on the side or rolled up into little burritos.

ENTOMATADAS DE CALABACITAS A LA MEXICANA

Zucchini Entomatadas

SERVES 4

FILLING:

2 tablespoons vegan butter or neutral oil, such as avocado oil, divided

¼ medium white onion, diced small

2 garlic cloves, minced

2 small Mexican zucchinis *or* 1 regular green zucchini, diced small

¼ teaspoon sea salt

⅛ teaspoon ground black pepper

2 ripe Roma tomatoes, seeded and diced very small

1 jalapeño pepper, seeded and minced

SALSA:

1 tablespoon neutral oil, such as avocado oil

¼ medium white onion, thinly sliced

2 cups Salsa Roja (page 75)

ENTOMATADAS:

5 tablespoons neutral high-heat oil, such as avocado oil

12 corn tortillas, store-bought or homemade (page 34)

Crema Mexicana (page 37) or store-bought vegan sour cream, for serving

Queso Cotija (page 38) or store-bought vegan feta, for serving

¼ bunch cilantro, chopped

¼ small red onion, thinly sliced

Entomatadas can be very closely compared to enchiladas although there is a distinct difference: enchiladas are smothered with a chile-based salsa and entomatadas, unsurprisingly, are made with a tomato-based salsa—it's right in the name of both! Entomatadas are typically not spicy, but they can be adjusted to have a kick with a touch of minced jalapeño if your spice-loving heart desires! Here I fill them with tomatoes and Mexican zucchini (see page 87). While they can be a great breakfast to enjoy on a weekend, they can also be a nice vegetable-packed weeknight dinner. Serve with a side of Frijoles Refritos (page 51) or Abuelita's Arroz Blanco (page 41).

---

1. To make the filling, melt 1 tablespoon butter in a large sauté pan over medium-low heat. Add the onion and sauté for 2 minutes. Add the garlic and sauté for 1 minute. Add another ½ tablespoon butter and half of the zucchini. Let the zucchini cook, undisturbed, for 2 to 3 minutes, until beginning to brown, then stir and cook for another 2 to 3 minutes, until the other side begins to brown as well. Season with the salt and pepper, then transfer the contents of the pan to a bowl.

2. Add the remaining ½ tablespoon butter to the pan and cook the remaining zucchini in the same way. Return the first batch of zucchini (plus the onion and garlic) to the pan and stir to combine. Add the tomatoes and jalapeño, stir to combine, and cook for 2 minutes. Turn the heat down to low to keep warm while you prepare the rest of the entomatadas.

3. To make the salsa, heat the oil in another large, deep sauté pan over medium-low heat. Add the onion and sauté for 2 to 3 minutes, until translucent. Add the salsa and cook for 2 minutes, then turn the heat down to low.

4. To assemble the entomatadas, heat the oil in a medium sauté pan over medium-high heat. Add a tortilla and fry for 20 to 30 seconds on each side, until golden and crispy but still pliable. Remove the tortilla from the oil with tongs and let the excess oil drip off, then drench the tortilla in the red salsa. Transfer the salsa-soaked tortilla to a serving dish. Spoon 3 tablespoons of the zucchini filling down one side of the tortilla, then fold in half or roll like a taquito. Repeat with the remaining tortillas and filling. To serve, spoon more salsa over the top, drizzle with crema, sprinkle with Cotija, and top with cilantro and red onion.

TOFU RANCHERO

SERVES 4

TOFU SCRAMBLE:

1 (14- to 16-ounce) package firm or medium-firm tofu

1 teaspoon garlic powder

½ teaspoon ground turmeric

½ teaspoon ground paprika

¼ to ½ teaspoon sea salt

¼ teaspoon black salt (kala namak; optional)

¼ teaspoon ground black pepper

7 tablespoons neutral high-heat oil, such as avocado oil, divided

¾ small white onion, ½ diced small and ¼ thinly sliced

¼ low-sodium vegetable broth

2 tablespoons tahini

3 tablespoons nutritional yeast

2 cups Salsa Roja (page 75)

12 corn tortillas, store-bought or homemade (page 34)

TO SERVE:

Frijoles Refritos (page 51), warmed

2 avocados, halved, pitted, peeled, and sliced

Cilantro sprigs

Queso Cotija (page 38) or store-bought vegan feta

Crema Mexicana (page 37) or store-bought vegan sour cream

In my family, only one person can be hailed as "la Reina de Huevos Rancheros" (the Queen of Huevos Rancheros), and that title is given to my sweet Tía Chela. Most of the women in my family are great cooks (it's said to run in our blood), but only a few have a genuine adoration for the act of cooking. You can especially see the passion my Tía Chela has for the craft in the hours she spends in the kitchen...it radiates in her spirit and you can undoubtedly taste the love in her cooking. So when you receive a recipe from her, you know it is going to be a good one. I was honored to use her recipe as the foundation for this "rancher-style" breakfast, swapping the traditional sunny-side-up eggs for tofu.

You can see why this would be a great, hearty breakfast to gear you up for a day of working on a ranch: golden, crispy fried tortillas are smothered in a rich and spicy salsa roja and refried beans, topped with a savory and hearty tofu scramble, and finished off with creamy avocado and crumbled Cotija cheese. Even if you're not setting out for a day of wrangling cattle, this still makes for an absolutely delicious breakfast.

---

1. Wrap the tofu in a kitchen towel or paper towel and squeeze for 10 to 15 seconds to remove the excess water. Put the tofu in a large bowl and crumble it into small pieces. Add the garlic powder, turmeric, paprika, salt(s)—if using black salt, use only ¼ teaspoon sea salt—and pepper and mix with your hands, ensuring that the tofu pieces are well coated with the spices.

2. Heat 1 tablespoon oil in a large nonstick skillet over medium-low heat. Add the diced onion and sauté for 2 minutes. Add the tofu and cook for 10 minutes, stirring frequently.

3. Meanwhile, whisk together the broth and tahini in a small bowl. After the tofu has cooked for 10 minutes and begun to brown, pour the broth mixture over the tofu scramble, then sprinkle with the nutritional yeast and give it another good mix. Cook for 2 minutes, then taste and add more sea salt or black salt if needed. Turn the heat down to low to keep warm while you finish the dish.

4. Heat a large, deep sauté pan over medium-low heat. Add 1 tablespoon oil and, once hot, add the sliced onion and sauté for 2 to 3 minutes, until translucent. Pour in the salsa and cook for 2 minutes, then turn the heat down to low.

5. Heat the remaining 5 tablespoons oil in a medium sauté pan over medium-high heat. Once the oil is hot, add a tortilla and fry for 40 seconds on each side, or until golden. Remove the tortilla from the oil with tongs and let the excess oil drip off, then place on a paper towel–lined plate. Repeat to fry the remaining tortillas.

6. Place 2 or 3 golden tortillas on each plate, spoon over some salsa, smother with warm refried beans, top off with tofu scramble, and pour more salsa on top. Garnish with avocado, cilantro, Cotija, and a drizzle of crema.

TACOS DE CHORIZO DE SOYA CON PAPA

Soy Chorizo–Potato Tacos

MAKES 8 TACOS

3 tablespoons neutral oil, such as avocado oil

2½ pounds Yukon Gold or russet potatoes, peeled or scrubbed and diced very small

¼ medium white onion, finely diced

3 garlic cloves, minced

1 (11-ounce) package soy chorizo (such as Cacique, El Burrito, or Reynaldo's)

½ teaspoon sea salt

8 corn or flour tortillas, store-bought or homemade (pages 34 and 30)

TO SERVE:

Crema Mexicana (page 37) or store-bought vegan sour cream

2 avocados, halved, pitted, peeled, and sliced

¼ white onion, finely diced

¼ bunch cilantro, chopped

Chorizo is a crispy, spicy, flavor-packed sausage that crumbles easily and is a natural protein choice for tacos. The fresh variety is a staple in Mexican cooking, although it originated in Spain, where it is found in cured form. You can easily find a soy version in Mexican (and American!) grocery stores. My Grandma Esther would often sneakily use soy chorizo in her cooking, and no one ever noticed. It has the same satisfying texture and rich savory flavor as the real deal...even my meat-loving dad often buys the soy version of chorizo for his cooking. This dish is a favorite for many in my family, especially my sister, Stefania. She studied in Europe and one thing she desperately missed from home was not her loving older sister (me) but instead, her weekly fix of savory, spicy tacos de chorizo y papa for breakfast. As she puts it, "I couldn't look at another croissant. I just really missed my chorizo y papa." Next time you need a taco that feels like a comforting hug and takes minimal time and effort, this is the move!

---

1. Heat the oil in a large skillet or sauté pan over medium heat. Add the potatoes, making sure not to crowd the pan (cook in batches if your pan isn't large enough, adding more oil as needed). Cook for 2 to 3 minutes on each side, until golden all around. Transfer to a paper towel–lined plate.

2. Turn the heat down to low, add the onion, and sauté for 1 minute. Add the garlic and sauté for 2 minutes.

3. Return the potatoes to the pan and turn the heat up to medium. Add the soy chorizo, using a spatula to break it apart and mix with the potatoes. Cook for 7 to 8 minutes, until the chorizo is slightly crispy and the potatoes are fork-tender. Season with the salt, then taste and adjust to your liking.

4. Heat a large skillet or comal over high heat. Add a tortilla and cook for 30 to 40 seconds on each side. Repeat to heat the remaining tortillas. To each tortilla, add a couple spoonfuls of potato and chorizo, then top with crema, avocado, diced onion, and cilantro.

CHILAQUILES DIVORCIADOS

Two-Salsa Chilaquiles

SERVES 4

⅓ cup neutral oil, such as avocado oil

12 corn tortillas, store-bought or homemade (page 34), cut into triangles

Sea salt

1 cup Salsa Verde (page 81)

1 cup Salsa Roja (page 75)

1 (8-ounce) package shredded plant-based mozzarella cheese

TO SERVE:

1 avocado, halved, pitted, peeled, and sliced

Crema Mexicana (page 37) or store-bought vegan sour cream

Queso Cotija (page 38) or store-bought vegan feta (optional)

¼ bunch cilantro, chopped

¼ medium white or red onion, thinly sliced

Chilaquiles—fried corn tortillas topped with salsa or mole, cheese, crema, and avocado—are kind of like breakfast nachos and make for the classic Mexican breakfast. It is a food that is tied to the tradition of intentional mornings and the indulgence of crispy fried tortillas smothered in toppings.

The options for serving here are endless, but traditionally you can make them with red or green salsa. On the days you can't seem to choose, or your household is split, chilaquiles divorciados is the solution. You've probably guessed this already, but "divorciado" means divorced, and this dish's name is a witty metaphor for the pairing of two salsas on one plate; together but, you guessed it, separated. To keep with the breakfast theme, eggs are a common addition for this dish, but for a plant-based alternative, Tofu a la Mexicana (page 59) makes for a great option, and I feel strongly that Frijoles Refritos (page 51) shouldn't be forgotten as a side to this dish.

---

1. Heat the oil in a large, deep sauté pan over medium heat. After a couple of minutes, add a tortilla triangle to the oil. If it sizzles, the oil is hot enough. If not, allow the oil to continue to heat, or slightly raise the temperature, and continue testing until the oil is hot enough. Once the oil is ready, add an even layer of tortilla triangles to the pan, being careful not to let them overlap. Fry for 1 minute on each side, or until golden. Using a spider, transfer the triangles to a paper towel–lined plate and very lightly sprinkle with salt. Add another batch of tortilla triangles and cook the same way. Continue until all the tortilla pieces are fried.

2. Warm the salsas in 2 separate small pots over medium-low heat for 5 to 7 minutes, until heated through.

3. Transfer all the fried tortilla triangles to a large skillet and heat over medium-low heat. Pour the green salsa over half of the skillet, carefully tossing the tortillas around to evenly coat, then pour the red salsa over the other half and do the same. Sprinkle both halves with an even layer of mozzarella cheese. Cover, turn the heat down to low, and cook for 3 minutes, or until the cheese is melted.

4. Top the chilaquiles with avocado, a drizzle of crema, Cotija cheese, a sprinkle of cilantro, and thinly sliced onion. For the full effect, I like to place the pan right on the table (making sure to use a placemat or trivet to protect your table from the heat) and serve directly from the pan.

❋ GUISADO DE PAPAS Y NOPALES ❋ EN SALSA ROJA CREMOSA

Potato and Cactus Creamy Tomato Stew

SERVES 6

4 Yukon Gold potatoes, peeled and cut into ½-inch cubes

1½ teaspoons sea salt, divided

4 nopales, thorns removed, cut into ½-inch squares

2 tablespoons neutral oil, such as avocado oil

½ large white onion, roughly chopped

5 ripe Roma tomatoes, roughly chopped

2 garlic cloves, roughly chopped

2 serrano peppers, stemmed

⅓ cup low-sodium vegetable broth, plus more as needed

⅓ cup pumpkin seeds

Nopal (prickly pear cactus) is grown throughout Mexico and is a vegetarian main character at most family gatherings. Beyond its role in vegetable-forward dishes, the nopal is an important symbol for Mexico due to its indigenous roots; it was even used medicinally by Indigenous Americans to help heal physical wounds. The plant is just as beneficial for our insides, as it is extremely nutritious, rich in antioxidants, vitamins, and minerals. It's the superfood of Mexican cuisine. Fresh nopales can be found in Mexican grocery stores.

This savory, comforting guisado (homey stew) is a wholesome way to begin your morning, consisting of nopales paired with starchy potatoes, gently simmered in a creamy pumpkin seed and tomato sauce. The blending of nuts and seeds into sauces is a pre-Hispanic culinary technique that I am always utilizing in my kitchen to give a dish not just a kick of plant protein but an added richness as well. Serve with your choice of either Tortillas de Maíz (page 34) or Tortillas de Harina (page 30), alongside Tofu a la Mexicana (page 59).

---

1. Put the potatoes in a medium pot and cover with about 3 inches of water. Add 1 teaspoon salt and bring to a boil over high heat. Cook for 8 minutes, then add the nopales and cook for an additional 7 minutes, or until the potatoes are fork-tender and the nopales have turned dark green.

2. Meanwhile, heat the oil in a large sauté pan over medium heat. Add the onion and sauté for 3 minutes. Add the tomatoes, garlic, and serrano peppers and sauté for 7 minutes. Transfer the contents of the pan to a blender, along with the broth, pumpkin seeds, and remaining ½ teaspoon salt. Blend on high until smooth. Pour the sauce back into the same pan and bring to a simmer over low heat.

3. Drain the potatoes and nopales and rinse under cool running water, then add to the sauce and mix to combine. Simmer everything together for 5 to 7 minutes. Taste and adjust the salt to your liking. The sauce should begin to thicken but still be smooth and slightly runny. If it thickens too much, you can loosen it up with a few more tablespoons of vegetable broth.

Salsas

SALSA ROJA

MAKES 2 CUPS

6 chiles de árbol, stemmed and seeded

1 serrano pepper, stemmed and seeded

½ medium white onion, ¼ left whole and ¼ thinly sliced

6 Roma tomatoes, halved

2 large garlic cloves, peeled

¾ cup low-sodium vegetable broth

½ teaspoon sea salt

2 tablespoons neutral oil, such as avocado oil

2 cilantro sprigs

Salsa roja is a classic Mexican condiment used for chilaquiles, huevos rancheros, and chiles rellenos. Every Mexican family has their own version of salsa roja, and my family recipe comes from my sweet Tía Chela. If an authentic salsa with depth, heat, flavor, and texture entices your taste buds, this will likely become a staple in your rotation of recipes.

I completely understand the excitement people in the United States have for some of the most iconic Mexican dishes I named above, although it pains me to see the lack of authentic ingredients and preparation in the salsas being used in restaurants or in online recipes. When a salsa is a key element of a recipe, most store-bought salsas will not do a recipe justice! This salsa requires only a handful of ingredients, like tomato, onion, garlic, serrano pepper, and chiles de árbol. Chile de árbol is a small dried pepper that packs a lot of heat. It can be found in the international aisle of your grocery store.

I have so many beloved memories of Sunday morning breakfasts where this salsa was the foundation of the dishes we drooled over. I invite you to be patient, present, and intentional when making this salsa to channel the same love as my Tía Chela!

---

1. Heat a medium sauté pan or skillet over medium heat. Once hot, add the chiles de árbol and serrano pepper. Cook the chiles de árbol for 10 seconds on each side, then transfer to a blender. Cook the serrano pepper for 1 to 2 minutes on each side, until charred, then add to the blender.

2. Add the whole onion piece, tomato halves, garlic cloves, broth, and salt to the blender and blend on high until smooth.

3. Heat the oil in a large, deep sauté pan over medium-low heat. Add the sliced onion and sauté for 2 minutes, or until translucent.

4. Pour the contents of the blender into the pan and turn the heat down to low. Simmer for 8 to 10 minutes, until the color of the salsa deepens. Add the cilantro sprigs and simmer for 2 minutes. Taste the salsa and add more salt if needed.

5. Use right away or store in a covered container in the fridge for up to 6 days.

SALSA DE MOLCAJETE

MAKES 2 CUPS

6 tomatillos, husked

3 Roma or heirloom tomatoes

4 garlic cloves, peeled

¼ medium white onion

2 serrano peppers, stemmed

Sea salt

¼ bunch cilantro, chopped

A molcajete (see page 19) is a traditional Mexican mortar and pestle made of volcanic rock, and it's an essential tool for making one of my favorite salsas. The porous texture of the molcajete gives the salsa a unique, jammy texture that is unlike that of a chopped or blended salsa. So incredibly flavorful, this condiment is best when spooned over Hongos Portobello y Soya Asada Tacos (page 134) or Taquitos de Yaca (page 136), or simply served with tortilla chips.

Using the molcajete brings me to a place of peace and calm and helps me stay present. It serves as a good reminder that things can feel more intentional when slowed down and unplugged. I always find myself playing one of my favorite Mexican artists, Natalia Lafourcade, and her *Musas* album to accompany me while I use my molcajete. So, give your blender a break and make this delicious salsa de molcajete.

---

1. Heat a large cast-iron skillet over medium heat. Put the tomatillos, tomatoes, garlic cloves, onion, and serrano peppers in the hot pan and roast on all sides until blackened. The garlic cloves will be done the quickest, after 1 to 2 minutes, so remove them first. The rest will take 2 to 3 minutes per side. (Alternatively, heat the oven to the highest broiler setting, put the vegetables on a rimmed baking sheet lined with aluminum foil, and broil on the middle rack for 1 to 2 minutes on each side, until charred.)

2. Put the roasted garlic in a molcajete, along with a good pinch of salt, and begin to mash well into a paste. Add the onion and peppers to the molcajete, breaking them apart and mashing well before adding the tomatillos and tomatoes and mashing everything together until you reach your desired consistency (I like a chunkier salsa). Add the cilantro and another pinch of salt and mix everything well with a spoon.

3. Use right away or store in a covered container in the fridge for up to 6 days.

SALSA MACHA

Mexican Chile Oil

MAKES 1½ CUPS

1 cup peanut oil, divided

8 to 10 garlic cloves, peeled

30 chiles de árbol (about ½ ounce)

½ cup roasted unsalted peanuts

2 tablespoons raw sesame seeds

1 teaspoon sea salt

Salsa macha's literal translation is "brave salsa," because you have to be brave to spoon this heat-packed condiment over your food! This oil-based salsa is infused with an aromatic blend of chiles, garlic, nuts, and seeds.

I fell deeply in love with this salsa after spending some time with family in the city of Oaxaca, where every restaurant had their own version. It was exciting to sit down at each meal to see what combination of ingredients and flavors were in the next salsa macha. Some were sweet, with the unique addition of dried fruits, while others contained a variety of nuts and seeds.

My version is nutty and smoky and has quite a kick, so put your brave face on...and proceed with caution as you add little spoonfuls (start small!) on your tacos, breakfast foods, or antojitos like Tlacoyos de Frijol (page 126) or Tetelas de Requesón de Almendras (page 113). I prefer to use peanut oil as the base, but avocado oil would work as well.

---

1. Heat ¾ cup oil in a medium pot over medium heat. Add the garlic cloves and cook, stirring continuously, for 15 to 30 seconds, until slightly golden. Remove the garlic cloves with a slotted spoon and transfer to a food processor or blender.

2. Add the chiles de árbol to the hot oil and stir for only about 10 seconds, letting them get slightly golden—they will become bitter if you let them cook too long. Transfer the chiles to the food processor or blender. Remove the pot from the heat and let the oil cool for 10 to 15 minutes.

3. Pour the cooled oil into the food processor. Pulse 8 times to break down the chiles.

4. Pour the remaining ¼ cup oil into the same pot and heat over medium-low heat. Once the oil is hot, add the peanuts and sesame seeds and cook, stirring constantly, for 10 to 15 seconds, until just golden. Carefully transfer the peanuts, sesame seeds and oil to the food processor or blender.

5. Add the salt and pulse a few times to break down the peanuts a bit. Pour the mixture into a jar. You can enjoy it right away, but the flavors will continue to develop as it sits for a couple days. Cover and store at room temperature for up to 6 weeks or in the fridge for up to 6 months.

SALSA ASADA

Roasted Salsa

MAKES 2 CUPS

"Ya probaste mi salsa?" (Did you try my salsa?) my dad asked proudly every week. There was rarely a moment when this salsa was not in our fridge, and if it was missing, we were all waiting for my dad to make the weekly batch so we could practically drown our food in it! This salsa was *the* salsa of our family, and because my dad made a new batch every week (with serrano peppers that are known for having very different levels of spice), it always varied in heat from medium to eye-watering spiciness. We endured many mornings of spice fumes hitting our throats and making us cough, but it was worth it for the gigantic jars of salsa that would fill our fridge. It's perfection with Quesadillas de "Atún" de Garbanzo (page 105), Tofu a la Mexicana (page 59), or tortilla chips. I hope this becomes a staple in your family as it is in ours!

---

1 tablespoon neutral oil, such as avocado oil

5 large ripe Roma tomatoes

½ small white onion, halved

1 large garlic clove, peeled

2 or 3 serrano peppers, stemmed

¼ bunch cilantro

¼ teaspoon sea salt

1. Heat the oil in a large cast-iron skillet over medium heat. Add the tomatoes, onion, garlic clove, and serranos and cook for 3 to 5 minutes, until charred and blackened on all sides.
2. Transfer the contents of the pan to a blender, along with the cilantro and salt. Blend on high until smooth. Taste and add more salt if needed.
3. Use right away or store in a covered container in the fridge for up to 6 days.

SALSA VERDE

MAKES 3½ CUPS

Mouthwatering: that's the word that comes to mind when I think of a homemade salsa verde. Also tangy, spicy, savory, acidic, and herbaceous. The key ingredient is tomatillos ("little tomatoes" in Spanish), a small, green or sometimes purple tomato with a papery husk. This bright, acidic salsa goes great with richer dishes like Tacos Dorados de Papa (page 150), Sopes (page 96), and Tamales Verdes (page 120). It varies from medium to hot depending on whether you use jalapeño or serrano peppers.

1½ pounds tomatillos, husked

2 jalapeño or serrano peppers, stemmed

3 garlic cloves, peeled

½ small yellow onion, halved

½ bunch cilantro

½ teaspoon sea salt

1. Put the tomatillos, jalapeños or serranos, garlic cloves, and onion in a medium pot. Cover with water and bring to a boil. Boil for 7 to 9 minutes, until the tomatillos turn a darker color.
2. Using a slotted spoon, transfer the vegetables to a blender. Let the ingredients cool in the blender for 15 to 20 minutes (optional, but resting helps reduce the bitterness of tomatillos).
3. Once cooled, add the cilantro and salt and blend until smooth. Taste and add more salt if desired.
4. Use right away or store in a covered container in the fridge for up to 6 days.

SALSA DE MANGO

Mango Salsa

MAKES 2 CUPS

2 or 3 medium ripe mangoes, peeled, pitted, and diced small

2 or 3 ripe Roma tomatoes, seeded and diced small

½ medium red onion, diced small

½ bunch cilantro, chopped

3 garlic cloves, minced

1 or 2 serrano or jalapeño peppers, stemmed, seeded, and diced small

¼ cup fresh lime juice (from about 2 limes)

2 tablespoons high-quality extra-virgin olive oil

½ teaspoon sea salt

1 avocado, halved, pitted, peeled, and sliced

My first memory of eating mangoes was at my abuelita's dining table. She cut both the cheeks off, then, using the tip of her knife, cut the most perfect little grid into the meat of the mango before popping the skin inside out and handing it to me. It was messy but the best way to eat all the flesh off the mango without anything going to waste. Nowadays I see viral videos of this exact way of cutting a mango and I always giggle to myself knowing the abuelitas in all of Latin America were the OG creators of this "mango cutting hack." When choosing a ripe mango, I always go for one that feels soft and smells sweet and fragrant. This salsa is sweet, savory, and spicy in all the best ways. A couple spoonfuls on Baja Palmitos Tacos (page 143) would be to die for, but you can't go wrong just serving it alongside a large bowl of tortilla chips.

---

1. Combine all the ingredients, apart from the avocado, in a large bowl. Mix, taste, and adjust the seasonings as you like. Wait until serving to top with sliced avocado.

2. Use right away or store in a covered container in the fridge for up to 6 days.

⁂ SALSA DE CHILE DE ÁRBOL ⁂

MAKES 2½ CUPS

35 chiles de árbol (about 0.6 ounce)

1½ pounds tomatillos, husked

½ medium yellow onion, halved

5 garlic cloves, peeled

¾ teaspoon sea salt

When I get asked if I would ever leave my hometown of San Diego, my answer is always no, at least not for good. I choose to live in a US border town, and I know it's exactly where I belong as a proud 200 percenter: 100 percent Mexican and 100 percent American. I especially feel this when I step foot in a San Diego Mexican grocery store. I see people who look like me, I hear my first language being spoken, and I see foods that bring me warm memories that feel like home. Aside from this significant feeling of belonging and comfort, a major advantage of Mexican grocery stores is the abundance of authentic, freshly made foods like tortillas and traditional Mexican staples like beans, rice, a hot bar of main dishes, and especially salsas. There is one particular salsa that my local Mexican grocery store makes daily in house called salsa caliente, or hot salsa, that I buy often and have served to my friends and friends. Each time, they can't get enough of it, to the point that every time the salsa would be praised, I grew a bit envious that I couldn't say "Thank you, I made it!" One day I politely (and of course in Spanish) asked the señora behind the counter what ingredients were in the salsa. She very kindly and willingly told me each ingredient used. She shared the "recipe" with me just as my abuelita or any of my tías would have relayed it to me, full of by-feel measurements...but I graciously took what I got and ran with it.

This *spicy* salsa is for people who like to feel their food as much as taste it. It packs a punch of flavor and heat and is perfection on anything your heart desires.

---

1. Put the chiles de árbol, tomatillos, onion, and garlic cloves in a large pot. Cover with water and bring to a boil over high heat. Boil for 7 to 9 minutes, until the tomatillos turn a darker color. Drain and transfer the vegetables to a blender, along with the salt. Blend on high for 1 minute. Taste and add more salt if needed.

2. Use right away or store in a covered container in the fridge for up to 6 days.

SALSA DE CALABACITA TAQUERA

Taquería-Style Zucchini Salsa

MAKES 2 TO 3 CUPS

- 5 tablespoons avocado oil
- 4 jalapeño peppers, stemmed and seeded if desired
- ½ small white onion, roughly chopped
- 4 garlic cloves, peeled
- 2 small Mexican zucchinis *or* 1 regular green zucchini, each cut into 4 pieces
- ¼ cup low-sodium vegetable broth
- 1 tablespoon fresh lime juice
- ½ bunch cilantro
- ½ teaspoon sea salt

This salsa is a creamy, blended, zucchini-based salsa served at taquerías across Mexico and the States. In fact, if you have ever asked for guacamole on your tacos at a taquería, there is a chance you've actually been served this salsa, and not guacamole. The taquería is the Mexican version of a fast food joint, serving primarily tacos but sometimes other dishes like tortas or enchiladas. They can be found on nearly every street corner in Mexico in the form of a food cart, stand, or small restaurant. They're also widespread throughout Southern California, Texas, and the Southwest, and they offer a great option for speedy meals that often include fresher ingredients and healthier options than regular American fast food spots.

This salsa is a tasty way to garnish tacos in a style that is similar to guacamole, but using more readily available and affordable ingredients. Mexican zucchinis are a heat-resistant variety of the squash that are slightly smaller than their cousins, with a lighter green skin flecked with gray—and they're a great option for home gardens, as they flourish all summer long. I make this salsa whenever my avocados aren't ripe enough; I especially like it spooned over Hongos Portobello y Soya Asada Tacos (page 134).

---

1. Heat the oil in a large sauté pan over medium heat. Add the jalapeños, onion, garlic cloves, and zucchini pieces. Pan-fry all the ingredients on each side until golden. Remove the garlic after 1 to 2 minutes per side; the jalapeños, onion, and zucchini will take about 4 minutes on each side.
2. Carefully transfer all the vegetables and the oil to a blender, add the broth, lime juice, cilantro, and salt, and blend on high until smooth. Taste and add more salt if desired.
3. Use right away or store in a covered container in the fridge for up to 6 days.

GUACASALSA

MAKES 2 TO 3 CUPS

2 tablespoons neutral oil, such as avocado oil

8 to 12 tomatillos, husked

½ medium white or yellow onion, roughly chopped

3 garlic cloves, peeled

2 jalapeño peppers, stemmed and seeded if desired

½ bunch cilantro

2 medium ripe avocados, halved and pitted

1 tablespoon fresh lime juice

½ teaspoon sea salt

This is a dream recipe for those who find themselves double-dipping their chip in guacamole followed by salsa verde. As the name hints, guacasalsa = guacamole + salsa. This dip/sauce does not necessarily have traditional roots, but guacamole and salsa absolutely do. The origins of guacamole date back to the 1500s, when the Aztecs of Mexico utilized avocado to make ahuaca-mulli, meaning avocado sauce. Around the same time, they combined tomatoes, chiles, and ground squash seeds to make the condiment that we know as salsa. While they might not have taken the extra step to mix the two, the modern combination of these two powerhouse condiments that are so beloved in all Mexican homes is a creation worth trying and embracing! It's creamy and slightly tangy and has a nice kick to balance all the flavors. Guacasalsa pairs well with Tacos Dorados de Papa (page 150), or just serve it with tortilla chips and crudités.

---

1. Heat the oil in a large cast-iron skillet over medium heat. Add the tomatillos, onion, garlic cloves, and jalapeños and cook for 2 to 3 minutes, until charred on all sides.

2. Transfer the vegetables to a blender, along with the cilantro, avocado flesh, lime juice, and salt, and blend on high until smooth. Taste and add more salt if needed.

3. Use right away or store in a covered container in the fridge for up to 4 days.

CHILE DE UÑA

Tomatillo Pico de Gallo

MAKES 3 CUPS

This bright, citrusy salsa recipe comes from my sweet, resilient Great Tía Pilla. Tía Pilla was my abuelita's best friend. They grew up together in a pueblo in Jalisco and shared an immense love for cooking. Tía Pilla was a super bright light and presence in my family. She lived her life to the absolute fullest through her love for tequila, traveling, and feeding her family. This salsa really embodies her essence, as it is bursting with freshness, brightness, and boldness, just as I would describe her. The fresh fruit juices are what really set this salsa apart. It was a major crowd pleaser whenever my tía would make it, and since she passed on a few years ago, I'm honored to bring this recipe back to life; it's admittedly hard to stop eating once you start. My mom shared with me her memory of when she got to experience this salsa for the first time in the early days of her marriage...everyone ran to the table and hovered over this bowl of salsa, devouring every last bit with tortilla chips. When she joined the family, she immediately asked my tía for the recipe.

1½ pounds tomatillos, husked and finely diced

⅓ cup fresh lime juice (from 2 to 3 limes)

¼ cup fresh orange juice

1 bunch cilantro, finely chopped

½ medium white onion, finely diced

½ teaspoon sea salt

1. Combine all the ingredients in a large bowl and mix well. Cover the bowl with plastic wrap and refrigerate for at least 3 hours or overnight before serving.
2. Store in a covered container in the fridge for up to 6 days.

ABUELITA'S SALSA DE PIÑA Y HABANERO

Grandma's Pineapple and Habanero Salsa

MAKES 2 TO 3 CUPS

My abuelita's pineapple-habanero salsa reminds me of her as a person: resilient and reliable but sweet and tender at the same time. Like my abuelita's personality, this salsa is perfectly balanced, and so delicious you always want more of it in your life. It has so much flavor it makes your taste buds sing! In our home we especially love it with tortilla chips.

---

1 or 2 habanero peppers, stemmed and seeded

4 garlic cloves, peeled

1 pineapple, peeled, cored, and cut into 1-inch-thick rings

½ teaspoon sea salt

¼ medium red onion, diced very small

⅓ bunch cilantro, chopped

1 teaspoon white vinegar

1 teaspoon extra-virgin olive oil

1. Heat an outdoor grill or stovetop grill pan over medium-high heat. Place the habaneros, garlic cloves, and half of the pineapple on the grill. Cook the habaneros and garlic for 1 to 2 minutes, until slightly charred on both sides, then transfer to a molcajete or food processor. Continue to cook the pineapple for an additional 3 to 4 minutes on each side, then transfer to a cutting board.
2. Add the salt to the molcajete. Using the pestle, mash the habaneros, garlic, and salt together until you reach a thick paste (or process if using a food processor).
3. Cut the grilled and fresh pineapple rings into small pieces. Add the pineapple to the molcajete, then add the red onion, cilantro, vinegar, and olive oil. Mix well with a spoon.
4. Use right away or store in a covered container in the fridge for up to 2 days.

ENTRADAS Y ANTOJITOS

Starters and Little Cravings

❋ SOPITA DE LENTEJAS ❋

Mexican Lentil Soup

SERVES 6

3 tablespoons neutral oil, such as avocado oil

1½ cups lentils, rinsed and drained

5 cups low-sodium vegetable broth

4 cups water, divided

3 ripe Roma tomatoes, halved

½ medium white onion, roughly chopped

3 garlic cloves, peeled

3 Yukon Gold potatoes, peeled and diced small

2 celery ribs, diced small

2 carrots, peeled and diced small

1 serrano pepper, slit lengthwise

¼ bunch cilantro

1 bay leaf

½ teaspoon sea salt

TO SERVE:

¼ bunch cilantro, chopped

2 limes, cut into wedges

Corn or flour tortillas, store-bought or homemade (pages 34 and 30), warmed

One of the warmest feelings from my childhood was hearing my mom or grandma ask, "Quieres sopita?" Sopita technically translates to "little soup," although the flavor of this soup is anything but little! When the diminutive "-ita" is added to the end of words in Spanish, it can be to describe something as small—or the smaller version of something large—although more often it is simply to add a nuance of affection, or to soften a word to be cute, somewhat like a nickname. Parents often add this "-ita" suffix to words for their children, although I can say that most Spanish speakers use it throughout their daily lives as well. To me, it just makes things feel sweeter and maybe makes our inner child happy. My dad calls me Alexita, and it's a term of endearment I happily embrace.

Every time I make a pot of my abuelita's sopita de lentejas, I am reminded that sometimes the simplest things in life are all we need to feel whole, taken care of, and nourished. This soup is the answer to a broken heart, a body that is sick, or a cold and gloomy day. It can make our hearts feel good while also nourishing our physical bodies, as lentils are a great plant protein and packed with vitamins and minerals.

---

1. Heat the oil in a large pot over medium heat. Add the lentils and cook for 1 minute, stirring frequently. Add the broth and 3 cups water. Simmer for 15 minutes.

2. Meanwhile, combine the tomatoes, onion, garlic cloves, and remaining 1 cup water in a blender and blend on high until smooth.

3. Pour the blended ingredients over the lentils, then add the potatoes and cook for 7 minutes. Add the celery, carrot, serrano, cilantro, bay leaf, and salt, turn the heat down to medium-low, and cook for 18 to 20 minutes, until the lentils are tender. Taste and add more salt to your liking.

4. Remove the bay leaf, garnish with the chopped cilantro and a squeeze of fresh lime, and serve with warm tortillas.

SOPES

MAKES 16 SOPES

SOPES:

2 cups masa harina (instant/ nixtamalized corn masa flour)

½ teaspoon sea salt

2 cups water

7 to 8 tablespoons neutral high-heat oil, such as avocado oil, divided

CHAYOTE:

3 tablespoons neutral oil, such as avocado oil, divided

2 chayote squash, peeled, pitted, and cut into ½-inch pieces

2 Roma tomatoes, diced small

½ medium white onion, thinly sliced

2 garlic cloves, minced

1 tablespoon dried rosemary

1 tablespoon dried oregano

1 teaspoon paprika

½ teaspoon sea salt

¼ teaspoon ground cumin

Juice of 1 lime

¼ bunch cilantro, chopped

Sopes is a traditional Mexican street food snack with a base of fried masa cake, smothered with refried beans, then typically finished with some if not all of the following toppings: a protein, salsa, lettuce, crema, and queso Cotija.

I associate these little bites of heaven with family, travel, and indulgence. One of my first memories of eating sopes was on vacation in Acapulco, in the southern state of Guerrero, while visiting family. I was around 10 years old, sitting around the table with all my cousins, when a large plate of these little masa cakes was placed in front of us. I wasted no time digging in, immediately exclaiming to my mom how much I loved them—she never made fried food at home, and agreed with me that they were quite the treat.

In Acapulco the sopes are often on the smaller side and are made simply, topped with beans, salsa, and sometimes cheese. In other parts of Mexico they are bigger and, in addition to refried beans, they're topped with chicken or beef, plus lettuce and crema. I love making a plant-forward version with a topping of flavor-packed chayote. This pear-shaped squash is hearty, something like a cross between a zucchini and potato, and a staple in Mexican cuisine. Beyond this recipe, it is great used in stir-fries, roasted as a side, or sliced thin into a salad.

---

1. To make the sope dough, in a large bowl, combine the masa harina and salt and mix well. Add the water ⅓ cup at a time, mixing well with your hands. Once all the water is added, mix with your hands for 7 to 10 minutes. Cover the masa with a damp paper towel and let sit while you prepare the chayote topping.

2. Heat 2 tablespoons oil in a large sauté pan over medium-low heat. Add the chayote and cook undisturbed for 2 to 3 minutes, then flip and cook undisturbed for 2 to 3 minutes on the other side. Add the remaining 1 tablespoon oil, followed by the tomatoes, onion, garlic, rosemary, oregano, paprika, salt, and cumin. Stir to combine, ensuring that the chayote is evenly coated with the spices, then sauté for 3 minutes. Add a splash of water, then cover, turn the heat down to low, and steam for 3 to 4 minutes, until the chayote is tender. Taste and adjust the seasonings to your liking. Add the lime juice and chopped cilantro and remove the pan from the heat.

(Continued)

(Continued)

TO SERVE:

Frijoles Refritos (page 51), warmed

½ head iceberg lettuce, shredded or thinly sliced

Crema Mexicana (page 37) or store-bought vegan sour cream

Salsa of choice, such as Salsa Verde (page 81) or Salsa de Chile de Árbol (page 84)

2 avocados, halved, pitted, peeled, and sliced

¼ bunch cilantro, chopped

2 limes, cut into wedges

3. To form the sopes, take a golf ball–size piece of dough and roll it into a ball between your hands, then flatten to make a disk about ¼ inch thick. (Alternatively, you can put the dough ball in a tortilla press and gently press down to create a thick tortilla.) Repeat to form the remaining sopes; you should get about 16.

4. Heat a large comal or skillet over medium-high heat. Add a sope and cook for 30 to 60 seconds on each side. Let cool for about 1 minute, then use your fingers to slightly round up the edges, forming a very shallow bowl; transfer to a plate. Cook the remaining sopes in the same way; once you get a rhythm going, you can alternate cooking the tortillas and crimping at the same time.

5. Heat 4 tablespoons oil in another large sauté pan or skillet over medium heat. Once hot, add a few sopes with the crimped edges facing up and fry for 1 to 2 minutes on each side, until golden. Transfer to a paper towel–lined plate. Fry the remaining sopes, adding more oil to the pan as needed.

6. To serve, ladle some warm beans onto each sope, then add some chayote, lettuce, a drizzle of crema and salsa, avocado slices, cilantro, and a squeeze of lime.

ESQUITES

SERVES 4

The most beloved street food in Mexico and in many border towns in the US is esquites: ears of corn slathered in butter, mayo, Cotija cheese, chili powder, and lime, eaten right off the cob.

Mexico has been growing corn for at least seven thousand years. Indigenous communities grew many varieties with different kernel sizes, colors, and textures, and a generally savory flavor. In the United States, however, corn is almost always sweet, and typically only two varieties of corn can be found—white or yellow—with medium-sized kernels that lean more juicy in terms of texture. The only time I was able to find corn in the US similar to Mexican corn was at my local farmers' market, where a Korean farmer was selling "Korean purple waxy corn," which he described so similarly to Mexican corn that I eagerly rushed home to make esquites. I closed my eyes with each bite and was transported to the streets of Coyoacán, enjoying esquites with my family. Ultimately, due to the differences in corn varieties and what's available in your supermarket, your experience eating esquites in the streets of Mexico will be different from what you can make in the States. Regardless, this dish is an exquisite snack or side for a cookout.

4 tablespoons vegan butter

½ white onion, diced small

2 garlic cloves, minced

4 ears corn, kernels cut off the cob

1 serrano pepper, slitted lengthwise (optional)

½ teaspoon sea salt

4 cups low-sodium vegetable broth

1 or 2 epazote sprigs (optional)

TO SERVE:

Mayonesa de Limón (page 36) or store-bought vegan mayonnaise

2 limes, cut into wedges

Chili powder or Tajín Seasoning

Queso Cotija (page 38) or store-bought vegan feta (optional)

1. Melt the butter in a large pot over medium heat. Add the onion and cook for 3 minutes. Add the garlic and cook for 1 minute. Add the corn kernels, serrano pepper (if using), and salt and cook for 5 minutes, stirring constantly. Add the broth and epazote (if using) and cook for 15 minutes.

2. Divide the corn into 4 small bowls. Serve with some of the broth and top with mayonnaise, lime juice, chili powder or Tajín, and crumbled Cotija (if using).

ALITAS DE COLIFLOR AL ESTILO CHIPOTLE

Chipotle Cauliflower Wings

SERVES 6

SAUCE:

2 tablespoons neutral oil, such as avocado oil

½ medium yellow onion, roughly chopped

4 garlic cloves, minced

½ cup canned chipotle peppers in adobo

¼ cup white vinegar

¼ cup water

1 teaspoon fresh lemon juice

¼ teaspoon sea salt

CAULIFLOWER:

2 cups neutral high-heat oil, such as avocado oil

1 cup all-purpose flour or gluten-free baking blend (such as Bob's Red Mill Gluten-Free 1-to-1 Baking Flour)

1 cup sparkling water

2 tablespoons cornstarch

1 tablespoon paprika

1 teaspoon garlic powder

1 teaspoon baking powder

½ teaspoon sea salt

1 large head cauliflower, cut into florets

Creating this recipe felt like I was honoring many parts of myself: the American in me, the Mexican in me, and the vegan in me. Buffalo cauliflower wings have become a staple in American vegan cuisine, and I wanted to satisfy that love for this flavorful plant-based dish while incorporating Mexican flavors. Plus, I've found that people go crazy for cauliflower when it's given the love and attention it deserves.

This sauce is tangy, acidic, and spicy with the help of chipotle peppers. Traditionally, American wings are paired with ranch, but since we're honoring the vegan Mexican American theme here, crema Mexicana is the sauce we're pairing these with! These will really impress friends and family at your next gathering, and they're a winning game day app.

---

1. First, make the sauce. Heat the oil in a large sauté pan over medium heat. Add the onion and sauté for 4 minutes, then add the garlic and sauté for 2 minutes. Transfer the sautéed onion and garlic to a blender, add the chipotles, vinegar, water, lemon juice, and salt, and blend on high until smooth; set aside.

2. To make the cauliflower, heat the oil in a medium pot or deep sauté pan over medium-low heat. Line a rimmed baking sheet with parchment paper.

3. Combine the flour, sparkling water, cornstarch, paprika, garlic powder, baking power, and salt in a medium bowl and whisk together until smooth. Dip a cauliflower floret into the batter, then use a fork to lift the cauliflower floret out and let the excess batter drip off. Transfer to the lined baking sheet. Repeat until all the cauliflower florets are coated in batter.

4. The oil should be 350°F. If you do not have a thermometer, you can dip the tip of a wooden chopstick into the oil: if tiny bubbles gather around the chopstick and come to the surface of the oil, it indicates that the oil is hot enough. Add one battered cauliflower floret to the oil and fry for 3 to 4 minutes on each side, until golden. Use a spider to transfer the floret to a paper towel–lined plate. Cut the floret in half to make sure it's tender and cooked. If it is still on the raw side, you'll know to cook the remaining florets a little longer, and perhaps at a slightly higher heat.

TO SERVE:

¼ bunch cilantro, chopped

Crema Mexicana (page 37) or store-bought vegan sour cream

Continue to test with individual florets, and once you reach the perfect heat setting and cook time, you can cook 4 or 5 cauliflower florets at a time, taking care not to crowd the pan.

5. Once all the cauliflower florets are fried, put them in a large bowl. Pour in the chipotle sauce and toss to evenly coat.
6. Garnish with chopped cilantro and serve with crema for dipping.

ENSALADA DE NOPALES

Cactus Salad

SERVES 5 OR 6

5 nopales, thorns removed, cut into ¼-inch squares

¼ cup coarse sea salt

2 small ripe Roma tomatoes, finely diced

½ small white onion, finely diced

3 tablespoons olive oil

¼ teaspoon ground black pepper

1 avocado, halved, pitted, peeled, and sliced

Queso Cotija (page 38) or store-bought vegan feta, for serving (optional)

Nopal is a cactus with leaves in the shape of a paddle, covered in large thorns that must be removed before cooking (they should be sold in the store that way). Much like okra, when cooked, nopal can become a bit slimy, and I find that most Mexicans either love or hate it for this reason. However, I'm almost positive that the technique I use to prepare this recipe will turn all my nopal haters to lovers, and if you're new to this special plant food, this recipe is a great introduction.

One day on a trip in the beautiful city of Puebla, I ordered an ensalada de nopales and corn tortillas to make tacos, as a vegan desperate for a plant-based option does. I was shocked by the unique texture and flavor of the nopales: they were a surprisingly bright green color and had little to no slimy residue. I couldn't leave the restaurant without asking the chef for his nopal secrets. He kindly shared that instead of traditionally boiling them, the key was to cure or "cook" the nopales in coarse sea salt. This process removes most of the slimy substance and renders the nopales plump and slightly crisp. For this salad, the little squares of nopales are then combined with the "Mexican flag"—tomato, onion, and cilantro—then seasoned simply with salt, pepper, and good-quality olive oil. Sliced avocado and homemade queso Cotija are a lovely addition. Serve as a topping for Tlacoyos de Frijol (page 126) or as a side for Hongos Portobello y Soya Asada Tacos (page 134).

---

1. Put the nopales in a large bowl, pour in the salt, mix well, and let sit for 10 minutes. After 10 minutes, mix the nopales vigorously again for 30 seconds.

2. Transfer the nopales to a strainer and rinse well under cool running water for 1 to 2 minutes, rubbing the leaves as you rinse; this will remove almost all the sliminess.

3. Return the nopales to the bowl, then add the tomatoes, onion, olive oil, and pepper and mix well. Top with the sliced avocado and crumbled Cotija cheese (if using).

QUESADILLAS DE "ATÚN" DE GARBANZO

Chickpea "Tuna" Quesadillas

MAKES 6 QUESADILLAS

"TUNA":

1 (15-ounce) can chickpeas, drained and rinsed

1 (14-ounce) can artichoke hearts or hearts of palm, drained and finely chopped

5 tablespoons Mayonesa de Limón (page 36) or store-bought vegan mayonnaise

¼ medium red onion, diced small

¼ cup pickled jalapeños, diced small

1 tablespoon fresh lime juice

1 teaspoon garlic powder

¼ teaspoon sea salt

¼ teaspoon ground black pepper

QUESADILLAS:

1½ teaspoons neutral oil, such as avocado oil

6 corn or flour tortillas, store-bought or homemade (pages 34 and 30)

2 (8-ounce) packages shredded vegan mozzarella cheese, divided

2 ripe avocados, halved, pitted, peeled, and sliced (optional)

Salsa Asada (page 80) or Guacasalsa (page 88), for serving

Crema Mexicana (page 37) or store-bought vegan sour cream, for serving (optional)

Quesadillas are to a Mexican home what I would imagine peanut butter and jelly sandwiches are to an American home: frequent and a go-to when the fridge and pantry are running low. I can honestly say that I ate a quesadilla every day of my life growing up. One day, my mom went into the kitchen to make what I thought was going to be a tuna sandwich. She popped open a can of tuna and prepared it with mayo and chopped jalapeños, but then instead of reaching for bread, she reached for the tortillas. She made a quesadilla, then opened it up to stuff it with the tuna. And that day, one of my favorite lunches was born. When I went vegan, I discovered that chickpeas make a great alternative to tuna, since they are high in protein and thus very satisfying. Chickpeas have a great texture when mashed and combined with a few other ingredients like artichokes or hearts of palm. My dad's Salsa Asada (page 80) goes nicely with these "tuna" quesadillas.

---

1. Put the chickpeas in a large bowl and mash with a fork. Add the artichoke hearts, mayonnaise, onion, picked jalapeños, lime juice, garlic powder, salt, and pepper and mix well. Taste, add a touch more mayo if needed to reach your desired consistency, and adjust the seasonings as needed.

2. To make the quesadillas, heat the oil in a large sauté pan over medium heat. Add a tortilla and heat for 30 seconds, then flip, add ⅔ cup cheese to half of the tortilla, and fold the other half over. Use a spatula to press down on the quesadilla and allow the cheese to melt, about 1 minute. Transfer the quesadilla to a plate. Open up the quesadilla and add about one-sixth of the "tuna" mixture, then close it back up. You can return it to the pan to heat the filling, but I like it as is! (Alternatively, you can add the tuna mixture to the quesadilla when you add the cheese, before cooking, although heating the quesadilla with only the cheese will allow it to melt more fully. You will need to cook the quesadillas for about 2 minutes on each side.) Repeat until all the quesadillas are cooked, adding more oil as needed.

3. Top with avocado slices, salsa, and crema to your liking. A nice little tip is to mix the crema and salsa for a great dipping sauce!

ENSALADA DE JÍCAMA

Jícama Salad

SERVES 10 TO 12

DRESSING:

5 tablespoons apple cider vinegar

3 tablespoons extra-virgin olive oil

2 tablespoons fresh lime juice

1 teaspoon red pepper flakes (optional)

½ teaspoon garlic powder

½ teaspoon sea salt

SALAD:

1 pound jicama, peeled and cut into small matchsticks

1 (1-pound) head green cabbage, cored and thinly sliced

2 medium cucumbers, cut into matchsticks

½ medium red onion, thinly sliced

1 jalapeño pepper, stemmed, seeded, and diced small

⅓ cup Japanese peanuts (see headnote), roughly chopped

This refreshing salad is a great dish to prepare ahead of time for a potluck or party, because unlike most salads, it stays crisp and gets even tastier after sitting in the fridge for a couple of days. This recipe is inspired by a salad my cousin Lizette makes often for family parties: a combination of shredded jicama, cucumber, and carrot, topped with fresh lime juice, chili powder, chamoy, and Japanese peanuts.

There aren't many fresh salads in Mexican cuisine, but we do love crispy, crunchy vegetables, from cabbage to jicama. Jicama is a starchy root vegetable that was valued by the Mayans and Aztecs, who mostly consumed it in its raw form. It has a similar texture to an apple but is a bit more savory, and it pairs beautifully with lime, chili powder, and—in this case—a simple vinaigrette.

The sneaky secret protein in this salad is a Mexican snacking staple that surprisingly isn't widely known in the US (yet!): Japanese peanuts, or peanuts coated in a salty-sweet, crunchy, soy sauce coating. These nuts did not originate in Japan but rather in Mexico, made by Japanese immigrant Yoshigei Nakatani, who arrived in Mexico City in 1932. Around the 1950s, Nakatani created a snack that connected him to his roots, and he began to sell the peanuts on the streets of Mexico City to help support his family. They quickly grew famous, and locals began to call them cacahuates japoneses. My favorite brand of Japanese peanuts, which can be found on Amazon and in Mexican markets in the US, is De La Rosa. This recipe calls for only ⅓ cup, but do yourself a favor and order multiple bags—you'll be hooked after one bite!

---

1. In a small bowl, whisk together all the dressing ingredients or combine the ingredients in a small jar, cover, and shake vigorously.

2. Combine the jicama, cabbage, cucumbers, onion, and jalapeño in a large mixing bowl.

3. Pour the dressing over the vegetables and mix well using your hands. Top with the chopped Japanese peanuts and enjoy right away, or hold off on adding the peanuts, cover the salad with plastic wrap, and refrigerate for up to 2 days to let the flavors marinate. Top with the peanuts when ready to serve.

CEVICHE DE PALMITO

Hearts of Palm Ceviche

SERVES 10

CEVICHE:

2 (14-ounce) cans hearts of palm, drained and diced small

1 large cucumber, peeled, seeded, and diced very small

2 ripe Roma tomatoes, seeded and diced very small

1 or 2 serrano peppers, stemmed, seeded, and diced very small

⅓ medium red onion, diced very small

½ bunch cilantro, finely chopped

½ cup fresh lime juice (from about 4 limes)

½ cup tomato juice

1 teaspoon garlic powder

½ teaspoon sea salt

TO SERVE:

2 ripe avocados, halved, pitted, peeled, and sliced

1 (10- to 12-ounce) bag tortilla chips *or* 10 tostadas

Mayonesa di Limón (page 36) *or* store-bought vegan mayonnaise (optional)

My family's "Mexican Americanness" really shone through when weekends would consist of football games and, instead of the classic game day appetizers being served, my dad would make a huge batch of ceviche for the family to munch on during the game. When I went vegan I really longed for the freshness of ceviche during the summer months and at family gatherings. My dad graciously shared his recipe with me, and I simply swapped the shrimp for our star ingredient, hearts of palm, which has a great flaky texture and subtle fish-like flavor. This recipe has become a go-to for serving to my seafood-loving family because it really embodies all the things we love in ceviche: crispness, spice, tang, and heart. It's just as well loved and quickly devoured as the bowl of fish or shrimp ceviche served alongside it at the family table!

---

1. In a large bowl, combine all the ceviche ingredients and mix well. Taste and add more salt if necessary. Cover with plastic wrap and chill in the fridge for 1 hour.

2. To serve, top with the sliced avocado and enjoy with tortilla chips for dipping, or spread a thin layer of mayonnaise on each tostada and add a generous amount of ceviche on top.

✲ CEVICHE ASADO DE HABANERO ✲

Habanero Roasted Ceviche

SERVES 8 TO 10

2 tablespoons neutral oil, such as avocado oil, divided

1 cup canned hominy, drained and rinsed

1 cup fresh or frozen white corn kernels

Sea salt

2 small Mexican zucchinis (see page 87) *or* 1 regular green zucchini, diced small

½ small red onion, finely diced

1 large mango, peeled, pitted, and diced small

¼ bunch cilantro, chopped

MARINADE:

¾ cup fresh lime juice (from about 6 limes)

2 oranges, peeled and white pith removed

2 garlic cloves, peeled

½ to 1 habanero pepper, stemmed

¼ bunch cilantro

TO SERVE:

10 tostadas *or* 1 (10- to 12-ounce) bag tortilla chips

2 avocados, halved, pitted, peeled, and sliced

Fresh ceviche is a staple of Mexican cuisine, but my husband and I were introduced to the concept of roasted ceviche at our wedding. This side dish is made of a combination of cooked and fresh ingredients contributing to a sweet, spicy, and tangy side dish that couldn't be easier to make. The addition of pan-fried hominy adds a nutty heartiness that is unexpected and so delicious! My husband and I got married in Mérida, Mexico, in 2022 and had the honor of having our wedding weekend catered by an incredible Oaxacan chef. Chef Sara made piña hominy ceviche tostadas for our Tornaboda, which is a get-together held the day after the wedding in Mexican culture. This unique take on ceviche quite literally revived my very exhausted body. The brightness and satisfying variety in textures and flavors brought me back to life after a long day of dancing and eating. This is my rendition of the ceviche my husband and I both fell in love with as very tired but exceptionally happy newlyweds the day after our wedding!

---

1. Heat 1 tablespoon oil in a large sauté pan over medium heat. Add the hominy and corn and cook for 4 to 5 minutes, until tender, then season lightly with salt. Transfer to a large mixing bowl.

2. Heat the remaining 1 tablespoon oil in the same pan over medium heat. Add the zucchini and cook for 5 to 6 minutes, until golden. Lightly salt the zucchini, then add to the bowl with the hominy and corn. Add the onion, mango, and cilantro to the bowl and stir to combine. Season with salt to taste.

3. Combine all the marinade ingredients in a blender and blend on high for 1 minute, or until smooth. Pour the marinade over the ingredients in the bowl and mix to combine. Taste and add more salt to your liking.

4. Cover and refrigerate for 2 hours. Serve on tostadas with sliced avocado, or with chips for dipping.

TETELAS DE REQUESÓN DE ALMENDRAS

Almond Cheese Turnovers

MAKES 10 TETELAS

ALMOND "REQUESÓN":

1 cup raw almonds

3 tablespoons neutral oil, such as avocado oil, divided

½ small white onion, roughly chopped

2 garlic cloves, peeled

½ cup water

2 tablespoons fresh lemon juice

½ teaspoon sea salt

MASA:

2 cups masa harina (instant/nixtamalized corn masa flour)

Sea salt

2 cups warm water

TO SERVE:

Salsa Asada (page 80) or Salsa de Chile de Árbol (page 84)

2 avocados, halved, pitted, peeled, and sliced

A few cilantro sprigs

The roots of tetelas lie with the Indigenous Mixtec people of Oaxaca, predating Spanish arrival in the area. They are that region's answer to empanadas, and usually consist of a thick corn tortilla, typically filled with black beans, that is then carefully folded into a little triangle pocket before being cooked until slightly crisp on the outside, with a soft masa inside. While the typical tetela happens to have a vegan filling of black beans, you can get as creative as your heart desires with the ingredients. For this recipe, I use a simple yet beyond scrumptious almond cheese that very closely resembles requesón, a Mexican cheese that is similar to ricotta but creamier and slightly more acidic. The almond "requesón" will be smooth and silky as you fill the tetelas, but once folded up into a triangle and thrown on the comal, the "cheese" magically firms up, transforming into a ricotta-like texture!

I was admittedly nervous serving these to my cheese-loving friends, but I will never forget the pleasant surprise on their faces as they bit into my tetelas. Serve with your favorite salsa, or even Mole Negro (page 159).

---

1. To make the requesón, put the almonds in a bowl, cover with boiling water, and let soak for 15 minutes. (Alternatively, you can soak the almonds overnight in room-temperature water.)

2. In a medium sauté pan, heat 2 tablespoons oil over medium-low heat. Add the onion and sauté for 3 minutes. Add the garlic cloves and cook for 3 minutes, until everything softens and begins to brown. Transfer the onion and garlic to a blender.

3. Once the almonds have soaked for 15 minutes, use a spoon to fish one out and remove the skin by squeezing the almond between your thumb and index finger. The skin should pop right off. If it does not, the almonds need to soak for a little longer. If the almonds are ready, drain them and remove the skins.

4. Add the almonds to the blender, along with the water, lemon juice, and salt, and blend on high for 1 minute. You may need a couple more tablespoons water if the mixture is chunky or having a hard time blending. Transfer the almond requesón to a small bowl.

(Continued)

(Continued)

5. To make the masa, in a medium bowl, combine the masa harina and a pinch of salt. Add the warm water a little at a time. Start with 1 cup, then add ½ cup, then the final ½ cup, mixing throughout with your hands. Once all the water is in, knead by hand for 8 minutes. Cover the masa with a damp paper towel and let sit for 10 minutes.

6. To make the tetelas, cut open a large ziplock bag or plastic produce bag, lay one piece across the bottom of your tortilla press, and set aside the other piece to lay over the dough. (Alternatively, you can use plastic wrap or parchment paper.)

7. Place a golf ball–size portion of masa in the center of the tortilla press. Cover with the top piece of plastic and gently press to form a tortilla about ¼ inch thick. (Alternatively, you can use your hands to roll the ball of masa between your palms, then flatten to make a disk about ¼ inch thick.)

8. Remove the top piece of plastic and add 1 to 2 tablespoons almond requesón to the center of the tortilla. Using the bottom liner, fold the tortilla from the upper left diagonally toward the center, then from the upper right toward the center, and finally from the bottom up toward the center to create a sealed triangle. Transfer to a plate. Repeat to form the remaining tetelas.

9. Heat the remaining 1 tablespoon oil on a comal or large nonstick skillet over medium heat. Working in batches as necessary, cook the tetelas for about 2 minutes on each side, until slightly golden.

10. Enjoy with salsa, sliced avocado, and a garnish of fresh cilantro.

SOPA AZTECA

Tortilla Soup

SERVES 4

8 tablespoons neutral high-heat oil, such as avocado oil, divided

4 ripe Roma tomatoes, halved

½ medium white onion, roughly chopped

3 garlic cloves, peeled

4 guajillo chiles, stemmed and seeded

1 ancho chile, stemmed and seeded

8 corn tortillas, store-bought or homemade (page 34)

6 cups low-sodium vegetable broth, divided

4 cilantro sprigs

½ teaspoon sea salt, plus more for seasoning

1 avocado, halved, pitted, peeled, and diced

1 lime, cut into wedges

Crema Mexicana (page 37) or store-bought vegan sour cream, for serving

Crunchy fried tortilla strips submerged in a rich broth with notes of spice, nuttiness, and smokiness, topped with avocado, fried dried chiles, and a drizzle of crema: in my opinion, this soup has it all. Complex flavors and textures, made with simple ingredients, make this a great soup for an easy weeknight dinner.

Sopa Azteca was created in the state of Tlaxcala sometime in the 1600s. This dish was inspired equally by the Spanish soup-making tradition and by pre-Hispanic culinary customs, with the focus on tortillas as the foundation of the dish. Thus sopa Azteca represents a coming together of the two dominant influences that together created modern Mexican cuisine.

---

1. Heat 1 tablespoon oil in a large sauté pan over medium-low heat. Add the tomatoes, onion, and garlic cloves. Cook the garlic until golden, 1 to 2 minutes on each side, then transfer to a blender. Continue to cook the tomatoes and onion for an additional 3 minutes on each side, until golden as well, then add to the blender.

2. Heat another 1 tablespoon oil in the same pan, still over medium-low heat. Add the chiles and cook for 15 seconds on each side. Set aside 1 guajillo chile and transfer the remaining 3 guajillos and the ancho chile to the blender. Use kitchen scissors to cut the reserved guajillo into ribbons and set aside for garnish.

3. Heat another 2 tablespoons oil in the same pan, still over medium-low heat. Tear 2 corn tortillas roughly into thirds and fry on each side for about 1 minute, until golden. Transfer to the blender.

4. Add 2 cups broth to the blender, then blend everything on high for 2 minutes, or until completely smooth.

5. Pour the blended mixture into a large pot, add another 2 cups broth, the cilantro, and salt, and bring to a simmer over medium-low heat. Cook for 15 minutes.

(Continued)

(Continued)

6. While the soup simmers, cut the remaining 6 tortillas into ½-inch-wide, 1-inch long strips. Wipe the sauté pan clean with a paper towel, then heat the remaining 4 tablespoons oil over medium heat. Add an even layer of tortilla strips to the oil and pan-fry for 30 to 60 seconds on each side, until golden, using a spatula to flip. Transfer the strips to a paper towel–lined plate, then repeat with the remaining tortilla strips until all are fried golden. Sprinkle lightly with salt.

7. Taste the soup and add more salt if needed. Serve hot with a generous handful of fried tortilla and chile strips, diced avocado, a squeeze of fresh lime juice, and a drizzle of crema.

✵ AGUACHILE DE LECHE DE COCO ✵

Coconut Milk Aguachile

SERVES 8

1 (15.5-ounce) can hominy

4 garlic cloves, peeled

½ teaspoon sea salt, divided

2 serrano peppers, stemmed, seeded, and roughly chopped

1 habanero pepper, roughly chopped (optional)

1 cup canned light coconut milk

1 cup fresh orange juice (from about 4 oranges)

½ cup fresh lime juice (from about 4 limes)

1½ tablespoons extra-virgin olive oil

3 (14-ounce) cans hearts of palm, drained and diced small

1 large cucumber (about 12 ounces), peeled in stripes and diced very small

½ large red onion, diced very small

½ bunch cilantro, chopped

2 avocados, halved, pitted, peeled, and diced

Tostadas or tortillas chips, for serving

Aguachile is traditionally a raw seafood dish with roots in the northwest region of Sinaloa. These days aguachile shows up differently depending on the region of Mexico where it's made. The version of aguachile my family enjoys consists of shrimp, cucumber, onion, and a chile-lime marinade.

This aguachile has a unique spin that was inspired by a chef I adore and admire, who catered our 2022 wedding in Mérida. Her aguachile had all of our guests quite literally licking their plates: it's light, citrusy, spicy, and flavorful, with a chile-lime and coconut milk marinade. Since then, we have made our own (vegan) version at home, and it takes us back to the most special day of our lives.

As in many other cultures, Mexicans take great pride in our traditions and sometimes become attached to the "authentic" way of preparing things. I see great value in this attitude, although I also really admire when creative chefs use their talents to think outside the box and create something new and enticing yet also familiar. It's a nice reminder that it is okay to use authentic ingredients and techniques as the foundation of a recipe, while also exploring innovative ideas, and that's exactly what this dish represents. Gracias, Chef Sara, por la inspiración!

---

1. Combine the hominy and garlic cloves in a large pot and cover with water. Bring to a boil over high heat and cook for 20 minutes. Drain in a colander and rinse under cool running water.

2. Remove the garlic and transfer to a molcajete or food processor, along with ¼ teaspoon salt, and mash or pulse to create a paste. Add the serrano peppers and habanero (if using) and mash or pulse really well into the garlic paste.

3. Transfer the paste to a large bowl, add the coconut milk, orange juice, lime juice, oil, and remaining ¼ teaspoon salt, and mix well. Add the hominy, hearts of palm, cucumber, red onion, and cilantro and mix well. Cover with plastic wrap and refrigerate for at least 2 hours or, if possible, overnight for even deeper flavor.

4. To serve, add avocado and enjoy with tostadas or tortilla chips.

❋ TAMALES VERDES ❋

Green Tamales

MAKES ABOUT 30 TAMALES

TAMALES:

About 40 corn husks

1½ cups vegetable shortening

2 teaspoons sea salt

2 teaspoons baking powder

6 cups masa harina (instant/nixtamalized corn masa flour)

6 cups low-sodium vegetable broth

¼ cup neutral oil, such as avocado oil

JACKFRUIT:

2 (20-ounce) cans green jackfruit in brine, drained and rinsed

½ medium yellow onion

2 garlic cloves, peeled

3 tablespoons neutral oil, such as avocado oil

¼ teaspoon sea salt

2 cups Salsa Verde (page 81), divided

ADDITIONAL FILLINGS:

1 pound Yukon Gold potatoes, peeled and cut into 1-inch matchsticks (like French fries)

2 poblano peppers, stemmed, seeded, and cut into 1-inch strips

TO SERVE:

Crema Mexicana (page 37) or store-bought vegan sour cream

Salsa Verde (page 81)

Tamales have been a point of cultural pride in Mesoamerican countries for thousands of years. They were created by Indigenous people around 8000 BCE, making tamales one of the oldest foods to exist today. Nowadays tamales are enjoyed by many Latin cultures, typically for special occasions like Christmas or other religious holidays.

Many gatherings for tamales began at my abuelita's home the moment the holiday season hit. My abuelita's love language was undoubtedly feeding her family, and one might say making three extra large pots filled with dozens of tamales is the ultimate form of love. One of my favorite tamales as a child, after Tamales de Elote (page 123), was salsa verde chicken tamales. The heartiness of the filling with a tangy acidic salsa is hard to beat in my book.

Here, jackfruit is stepping in for the chicken, to make these nostalgic tamales come to life. A young unripe jackfruit contains pods of fruit that are savory and pull apart similarly to chicken or pulled pork. I recommend buying young jackfruit in brine, often found in a can or pouch. Similar to chicken, jackfruit takes on flavors really well.

If you take anything away from the veganized elements of this recipe, let it be the masa. One holiday season I set out to create a masa that was free of lard but still packed with flavor and moisture, and after lots of trial and error, I found that vegetable shortening was the best lard replacement, making for the softest, most tender masa.

Over the past three years, I have had the honor of teaching hundreds of people around the world how to make tamales via a virtual cooking class. My favorite type of feedback comes from Mexican families sharing that they replaced their family masa recipe with my masa recipe, for all the holiday seasons onward. The variations of fillings are endless, but with this masa as a foundation, you're bound to make some of the best tamales of your life.

---

1. Sort through the corn husks and toss any that have little holes or marks. I always encourage buying more husks than you need to account for the bad ones in a batch. Put the good corn husks in a large bowl and cover with room-temperature water. Place a bowl or plate on top so that the husks are fully submerged. Soak for at least 1 hour or overnight.

(Continued)

(Continued)

2. To make the masa, put the vegetable shortening in the bowl of a stand mixer and beat until very light, about 1 minute. (Alternatively, you can use a hand mixer or whisk.) Add the salt and baking powder and mix until combined. Alternate adding the masa harina and broth, about ⅓ cup at a time, mixing well after each addition. Continue beating until the dough is fluffy, then add the oil and beat for another 3 to 4 minutes. Cover the masa with plastic wrap while you prepare the jackfruit.

3. Put the jackfruit in a large bowl and remove the soft seed inside each piece, then discard. Transfer the jackfruit to a medium pot. Cover with water (about 5 inches above the jackfruit) and add the onion and garlic cloves. Bring to a boil over medium heat and cook for 30 minutes. Drain in a colander and rinse under cool running water. Discard the onion and garlic. Put the jackfruit in the center of a thin kitchen towel or in a nut milk bag and form into a bundle. Squeeze to press out all the liquid. Transfer the jackfruit to a cutting board and roughly chop.

4. Heat the oil in a large sauté pan over medium-low heat. Add the jackfruit and cook, undisturbed, for 3 minutes, or until golden on one side, then flip and brown the other side. Season with the salt. Pour in 1½ cups salsa, mix well, turn the heat down to low, and cook for 15 to 20 minutes. The mixture will begin to thicken and the jackfruit will become more tender. Taste and add salt to your liking, then transfer the jackfruit mixture to a bowl.

5. To assemble the tamales, drain the corn husks and pat dry with a paper towel or kitchen towel. Lay out a corn husk with the tapering end toward you. About 2 inches up from the bottom of the husk, spread 3 to 4 tablespoons masa into a 2- to 3-inch square, about ¼ inch thick. In the center of the masa square, add a heaping spoonful of the jackfruit mixture, one piece of potato, and one piece of poblano pepper.

6. Fold one side of the husk over the filling, then fold the other side over as though you're wrapping a present, and finally fold up the tapering bottom. Set aside with the folded ends down so it stays shut as you assemble the remaining tamales (about 30).

7. Pour an inch or two of water into a large pot and set a steamer over it. Make sure the water comes up to right below the steamer. Bring the water to a boil. Place the tamales in the steamer, standing up. Cover with any remaining corn husks, turn the heat down to medium-low, cover, and steam for 1½ hours. Add a few splashes of water to the pot if needed throughout the cooking process.

8. Turn off the heat and let the tamales sit for 1 hour to firm up. You will know the tamales are ready when they can be easily separated from the husks.

9. Serve with crema and salsa.

TAMALES DE ELOTE

Sweet Corn Tamales

MAKES ABOUT 25 TAMALES

About 40 corn husks

2 cups fresh or thawed frozen corn kernels

2 tablespoons vegan butter, softened

1 to 4 tablespoons cane sugar

¾ teaspoon sea salt

¾ to 1 cup masa harina (instant/nixtamalized corn masa flour)

Lechera (page 203) or Cajeta (page 202), if making sweet tamales

Crema Mexicana (page 37) or salsa of choice, if making savory tamales

Tamales de elote is a traditional recipe from the Mexican states of Michoacán and Guerrero. As a little girl I loved these tamales because they are slightly sweet, fluffy, and so flavorful—my deep love of corn was fully satisfied by these little pillows of corn-infused dough. What sets these apart from traditional tamales is the absence of a filling; the main attraction here is the masa. The masa is typically a mixture of fresh and nixtamalized corn, butter, a touch of sugar, and salt. Some family recipes also add cheese, milk, and sweetened condensed milk. Personally, I think simple is best when it comes to tamales de elote, as I really appreciate the corn shining through. You can elevate the sweetness by serving with a cup of hot chocolate and a drizzle of Lechera (page 203) or focus on the savory with a spoonful of Salsa Verde (page 81) and a dollop of Crema Mexicana (page 37).

---

1. Sort through the corn husks and toss any that have little holes or marks. I always encourage buying more husks than you need to account for the bad ones in a batch. Put the good corn husks in a large bowl and cover with room-temperature water. Place a bowl or plate on top so that the husks are fully submerged. Soak for at least 1 hour or overnight.

2. To make the masa, combine the corn, butter, cane sugar (1 tablespoon if making savory tamales, or all 4 tablespoons if making sweet tamales), and salt in a food processor or blender. Blend on high for 30 seconds, or until you achieve a smooth consistency but with some small pieces of corn remaining. Add ¾ cup masa harina and blend again for 1 minute. It should have the consistency of a brownie batter. If the mixture seems too wet, add up to ¼ cup more masa harina.

3. To assemble the tamales, drain the corn husks and pat dry with a paper towel or kitchen towel. Lay out a corn husk with the tapering end toward you. About 2 inches up from the bottom of the husk, spread 3 to 4 tablespoons masa into a 2- to 3-inch square, about ¼ inch thick. Fold one side of the husk over the filling, then fold the other side over as though you're wrapping a present, and finally fold up the tapering bottom. Set aside with the folded ends down so it stays shut as you assemble the remaining tamales (about 25).

(Continued)

(Continued)

4. Pour an inch or two of water into a large pot and set a steamer over it. Make sure the water comes up to right below the steamer. Bring the water to a boil. Place the tamales in the pot, standing up. Cover with any remaining corn husks, turn the heat down to medium-low, cover, and steam for 1½ hours. Add a few splashes of water to the pot if needed throughout the cooking process.

5. Turn off the heat and let the tamales sit for 1 hour to firm up. You will know the tamales are ready when they can be easily separated from the husks.

6. For sweet tamales serve with lechera or cajeta, and for savory tamales serve with crema or salsa.

⁂ TLACOYOS DE FRIJOL ⁂

Bean Turnovers

MAKES 9 TO 12 TURNOVERS

2 cups masa harina (instant/nixtamalized corn masa flour)

Sea salt

2 cups warm water

1 to 2 cups Frijoles Refritos (page 51)

Neutral oil, such as avocado oil, for frying

TO SERVE:

Salsa de Chile de Árbol (page 84)

Ensalada de Nopales (page 102)

Crema Mexicana (page 37) or store-bought vegan sour cream

Queso Cotija (page 38) or store-bought vegan feta

When I was 23 years old, I packed my bags and moved to Mexico City for 6 weeks. I was feeling lost and thought I could find myself in a place that made me feel so much comfort and connection to my roots. One of the dishes that helped me reconnect was the tlacoyo, another plant-forward, pre-Hispanic creation. A thick, crispy-on-the-outside, soft-on-the-inside masa tortilla filled with refried beans and often topped with ensalada de nopales, salsa, and queso Cotija, tlacoyos were one of the dishes that brought me back to my love for my people and our cuisine. *Note: If you'd like to add squash blossoms, as pictured, follow the preparation instructions in the Tortillas de Maíz recipe on page 34, adding the blossoms in step 3 of this recipe.*

---

1. In a medium bowl, combine the masa harina and a pinch of salt. Add the warm water a little at a time. Start with 1 cup, then add ½ cup, then the final ½ cup, mixing throughout with your hands. Once all the water is in, knead by hand for 8 minutes. Cover the masa with a damp paper towel and let sit for 10 minutes.

2. Cut open a large ziplock bag or plastic produce bag, lay one piece across the bottom of your tortilla press, and set aside the other piece to lay over the dough. (Alternatively, you can use plastic wrap or parchment paper.)

3. Place a golf ball–size portion of masa in the center of the tortilla press. Cover with the top piece of plastic and gently press to form a tortilla about ¼ inch thick. (Alternatively, you can use your hands to roll the ball of masa between your palms, then flatten to make a disk about ¼ inch thick.)

4. Remove the top piece of plastic and add 1 heaping tablespoon refried beans to the center of the disk and fold in half (kind of like a dumpling), then use your hands to form a flat oval. Repeat to form the remaining tlacoyos.

5. Heat a drizzle of oil in a large skillet or comal over medium-low heat. Working in batches, cook the tlacoyos for about 2 minutes on each side, until golden, adding more oil as needed. Keep the cooked tlacoyos warm under a kitchen towel while you cook the rest.

6. Serve with your choice of toppings.

TORTITAS DE GARBANZOS Y PAPAS

Chickpea and Potato Patties

MAKES 9 PATTIES

2 (1-pound) Yukon Gold potatoes, peeled and cut into 1-inch cubes

1 tablespoon neutral oil, such as avocado oil

¼ medium yellow onion, diced small

2 garlic cloves, minced

1 (15-ounce) can chickpeas, drained (reserve ¼ cup liquid) and rinsed

½ cup bread crumbs or gluten-free bread crumbs

½ teaspoon garlic powder

½ teaspoon sea salt, plus more for seasoning

¼ teaspoon ground black pepper

5 to 6 tablespoons neutral high-heat oil, such as avocado oil

TO SERVE:

¼ bunch cilantro, chopped

Crema Mexicana (page 37) or store-bought vegan sour cream

Salsa Verde (page 81)

Potatoes and chickpeas are some of most accessible and inexpensive plant foods, making these delicious little patties an affordable dish to fall back on when you're running low on fresh groceries at the end of the week, but they're so tasty they're also a great option for entertaining friends and family. My abuelita would make tortitas de papas frequently, and while I love her recipe as is, the addition of chickpeas gives the patties a nice texture and a little kick of plant protein, making them more satisfying as a meal. These are lovely paired with crema and salsa verde, just how my abuelita would serve them.

---

1. Put the potatoes in a medium pot and cover with water. Bring to a boil over high heat and cook for 15 to 17 minutes, until fork-tender.

2. Meanwhile, heat the oil in a medium sauté pan over medium-low heat. Add the onion and sauté for 3 minutes, then add the garlic and sauté for 1 minute. Remove from the heat.

3. Drain the potatoes. Transfer the potatoes to a medium bowl and mash with a fork or potato masher until mostly smooth with some small lumps. Add the chickpeas and reserved liquid, cooked onion and garlic, bread crumbs, garlic powder, salt, and pepper and mix well.

4. Scoop out a golf ball–size portion of the mixture and form into a ¼-inch-thick patty. Repeat to make 9 patties.

5. Heat 5 tablespoons oil in a large sauté pan or skillet over medium heat. Working in batches, gently add the patties and fry until nicely browned, about 2 minutes on each side, adding more oil as needed. Transfer the patties to a plate and lightly season with salt.

6. To serve, top with the cilantro, crema, and salsa.

❋ RAJAS CON CREMA ❋

Roasted Poblano Peppers in Cream Sauce

SERVES 5 OR 6

1 cup raw cashews

5 poblano peppers (sometimes labeled pasilla peppers)

2 tablespoons neutral oil, such as avocado oil

1 tablespoon vegan butter or additional oil

1 small white onion, thinly sliced

3 garlic cloves, minced

½ teaspoon sea salt, divided

1 pound cremini mushrooms, thinly sliced

2 cups water

Rajas con crema is always part of our family gatherings and always on my brother Alec's plate; it's his absolute favorite. He is a very passionate and expressive person, and it's sweet seeing how this dish lights him up. Most families use corn and peppers, but my tías make my abuelita's recipe, which replaces the corn with mushrooms. The cream in my rendition of the recipe is made of cashews for the silkiest, smoothest, most luscious sauce. I once made this for a friend who had never had or heard of this dish, and he said, "The best way to describe how I feel while eating this is 'home.'" Enjoy with flour or corn tortillas and a side of Arroz Verde (page 47) or Abuelita's Arroz Blanco (page 41).

---

1. Put the cashews in a bowl, cover with boiling water, and let soak for 15 minutes. (Alternatively, you can soak the cashews overnight in room-temperature water.)

2. Meanwhile, roast the poblano peppers on an open flame for 1 to 2 minutes, until charred on all sides. (Alternatively, heat the oven to the highest broiler setting, put the poblanos on a rimmed baking sheet lined with aluminum foil, and broil on the middle oven rack for 1 to 2 minutes on each side, until charred.) Transfer the poblano peppers to a bowl, cover with plastic wrap, and let sit for 10 minutes to release steam.

3. Heat the oil and butter in a large sauté pan over medium-low heat. Add the onion and cook for 3 minutes, then add the garlic and ¼ teaspoon salt and cook for 1 minute. Add the mushrooms and cook, undisturbed, for 2 to 3 minutes, until golden, then stir so they cook on the other side for 3 minutes, or until golden. Season with the remaining ¼ teaspoon salt and continue to cook, stirring, for another 2 minutes.

4. Remove the charred skin, stems, inner ribs, and seeds from the poblano peppers. Cut into thin, 1-inch-long strips. Add the poblano peppers to the mushroom mixture, turn the heat down to low, and sauté for 3 minutes.

5. Meanwhile, drain the cashews and transfer to a blender. Add the fresh water and blend on high for 1 minute, or until smooth.

6. Pour the crema over the mushrooms and poblano peppers, mix, and simmer for 5 to 6 minutes. Taste and add salt to your liking.

Tacos

✵ HONGOS PORTOBELLO Y SOYA ASADA TACOS ✵

Portobello Mushroom and Roasted Soy Tacos

MAKES 10 TACOS

MARINADE:

1 cup fresh orange juice (from about 4 oranges)

½ cup fresh lime juice (from about 4 limes)

½ cup low-sodium soy sauce

⅓ cup low-sodium vegetable broth

¼ cup extra-virgin olive oil

2 tablespoons white wine vinegar or apple cider vinegar

¼ medium white onion, thinly sliced

¼ bunch cilantro, chopped

3 canned chipotle peppers in adobo, finely chopped

1½ tablespoons cane sugar

1 teaspoon dried oregano

1 teaspoon garlic powder

½ teaspoon ground cumin

½ teaspoon chili powder

¼ teaspoon ground black pepper

TACO FILLING:

1 (8-ounce) package TVP, such as Butler Soy Curls, *or* 4 portobello mushroom caps, sliced ½ inch thick

6 tablespoons neutral oil, such as avocado oil, divided

These tacos are inspired by special memories of weekend carne asadas—the Mexican version of a cookout—prepared by my dad. These gatherings occur not just to celebrate a holiday, but also to celebrate family and life, which many Mexican families do often. During these weekend get-togethers, the main dish itself was always prepared by my dad. For the meat eaters, this meant marinated meat that is grilled, chopped, and served with tortillas, salsa, guacamole, rice, and beans prepared by my mother or other relatives. For vegans and vegetarians, portobello mushrooms or TVP (see page 22) soak up the savory, citrusy marinade beautifully and will satisfy the carnivores and herbivores alike at your next carne asada. For the best results, marinate the TVP or mushrooms overnight.

---

1. In a large bowl, whisk together all the marinade ingredients.
2. If using TVP, put the TVP in a large bowl and cover with hot water. Place a bowl or plate on top so that the TVP is fully submerged. Soak for 30 minutes. Drain in a colander, then squeeze the TVP to release more water.
3. Add the TVP or mushrooms to the bowl of marinade and mix to combine. Cover with plastic wrap and refrigerate for at least 2 hours or, preferably, overnight.
4. Heat 2 tablespoons oil in a large sauté pan or skillet over medium-low heat. Use a slotted spoon to transfer about a third of the marinated TVP or mushrooms to the pan, making sure the pieces do not overlap. Cook for 4 to 5 minutes on each side, until golden and charred, flipping with a spatula. Add ¼ cup of the marinade, mix, and cook for 1 minute. Transfer the contents of the pan to a medium bowl.
5. Repeat to cook the remaining 2 batches of TVP or mushrooms, using 2 tablespoons oil for each batch. Once the last batch is cooked, return everything to the pan and stir to combine. Remove the pan from the heat.
6. Heat a medium skillet or comal over high heat. Add a tortilla and heat for 30 to 40 seconds on each side. Repeat to heat the remaining tortillas. Add about ¼ cup of the TVP or mushroom mixture to each tortilla, top with finely diced onion, chopped cilantro, a squeeze of fresh lime, and salsa of your choice.

TO SERVE:

10 corn or flour tortillas, store-bought or homemade (pages 34 and 30)

¼ white onion, finely diced

¼ bunch cilantro, finely chopped

4 limes, cut into wedges

Guacasalsa (page 88) or Salsa de Calabacita Taquera (page 87)

TAQUITOS DE YACA

Jackfruit Rolled Tacos

MAKES 10 ROLLED TACOS

2 (20-ounce) cans green jackfruit in brine, drained and rinsed

1 medium yellow or white onion, ½ left whole and ½ thinly sliced

4 garlic cloves, peeled, 2 left whole and 2 minced

4 tablespoons plus ⅓ cup neutral high-heat oil, such as avocado oil, divided

Sea salt and ground black pepper

2 cups Salsa Verde (page 81), plus more for serving

10 corn or flour tortillas, store-bought or homemade (pages 34 and 30)

2 avocados, halved, pitted, peeled, and sliced

¼ to ½ bunch cilantro, chopped

Crema Mexicana (page 37) or store-bought vegan sour cream, for serving

I feel like it was just yesterday that I was coming home from middle school hungry and eager to prepare my favorite after school snack: taquitos with Esquites (page 99). Also known as rolled tacos or flautas, taquitos are the most delectable little handheld food, made of crispy tortillas with a meaty filling and topped with crema, salsa, and avocado. This version is stuffed with green jackfruit, a plant-based alternative to shredded meat. This unique fruit is native to Asia, Africa, and South America and, when consumed in its unripe form, has a texture so similar to shredded chicken I have even fooled some non-veg friends and family!

---

1. Put the jackfruit in a large bowl and remove the soft seed inside each piece, then discard. Transfer the jackfruit to a medium pot. Cover with water (about 5 inches above the jackfruit) and add the whole onion piece and whole garlic cloves. Bring to a boil over medium heat and cook for 30 minutes. Drain in a colander and rinse under cool running water. Discard the onion and garlic. Put the jackfruit in the center of a thin kitchen towel or in a nut milk bag and form into a bundle. Squeeze to press out all the liquid. Transfer the jackfruit to a cutting board and roughly chop.

2. Heat 3 tablespoons oil in a large sauté pan over medium-low heat. Add the jackfruit and cook, undisturbed, for 3 to 4 minutes, until golden on one side, then stir and lightly season with salt and pepper. Transfer the jackfruit to a bowl.

3. Heat 1 tablespoon oil in the same pan over medium-low heat. Add the sliced onion and sauté for 3 minutes, then add the minced garlic and sauté for 1 minute. Add 1 cup salsa verde, mix well, and cook for 5 minutes, or until the salsa thickens. Return the jackfruit to the pan and stir to combine, then add the remaining 1 cup salsa verde and mix everything together. Cook for 5 minutes, then remove the pan from the heat.

4. Heat a comal or medium skillet over high heat. Add a tortilla and heat for 30 to 40 seconds on each side, then transfer to a tortilla holder or wrap in a kitchen towel. Repeat to heat the remaining tortillas.

5. Heat the remaining ⅓ cup oil in a large, deep sauté pan over medium heat.

6. To form the taquitos, add 2 spoonfuls of the jackfruit mixture to one half of each warmed tortilla, then roll up tightly to form a cigar shape.

7. Working in batches, add the taquitos to the oil, seam side down, and fry for 2 to 3 minutes on each side, until golden. Using tongs, transfer the taquitos to a paper towel–lined plate.

8. Top the taquitos with salsa verde, avocado, cilantro, and crema.

TACOS DORADOS DE PICADILLO

Crispy "Beef" Tacos

MAKES 12 TACOS

FILLING:

2 tablespoons neutral oil, such as avocado oil

½ medium white onion, diced small

3 garlic cloves, minced

2 large carrots, peeled and diced small

2 Yukon Gold potatoes, peeled and diced small

½ cup low-sodium vegetable broth

1 (12-ounce) package plant-based ground meat (such as Impossible or Beyond Meat)

¼ teaspoon sea salt

SALSA:

1 tablespoon neutral oil, such as avocado oil

2 ripe Roma tomatoes

¼ medium white onion

1 serrano or jalapeño pepper, stemmed and seeded

2 garlic cloves, peeled

¼ cup low-sodium vegetable broth

¼ bunch cilantro

¼ teaspoon sea salt

TACOS:

12 corn tortillas, store-bought or homemade (page 34)

6 to 8 tablespoons neutral high-heat oil, such as avocado oil

Guacasalsa (page 88), for serving

"Taco night" for many across the United States consists of an Americanized idea of Mexican food: ground beef cooked with a packaged seasoning mix, taco shells, lettuce, tomato, and sour cream. Let's just say that if you're reading this and have enjoyed a similar meal, you will be blown out of the water by the authentic version. These tacos were a favorite of mine as a kid. I remember watching my Tía Chela making them and getting so excited for the meal to come because they felt like such a treat. The secret here is using salsa to season your meat, rather than dried herbs and spices, which creates much juicier, deeper flavor.

---

1. To make the filling, heat the oil in a large sauté pan over medium-low heat. Add the onion and sauté for 2 minutes, then add the garlic, carrots, and potatoes and sauté for 4 minutes. Turn the heat down to low and add the broth. Cover and steam for 10 to 12 minutes, until the vegetables are fork-tender. Add the ground meat and cook, using a spatula to break up any large clumps, for 7 to 10 minutes, until browned. Season with the salt.

2. Meanwhile, make the salsa. Heat the oil in a large skillet or sauté pan over medium heat. Add the whole tomatoes, onion quarter, serrano or jalapeño pepper, and garlic cloves and cook for 2 to 4 minutes on each side, until blackened and charred (the garlic might char more quickly, after 2 to 3 minutes total). Transfer the contents of the pan to a blender. Add the broth, cilantro, and salt and blend on high until smooth.

3. Add the salsa to the meat and vegetable mixture and stir to combine. Cook for 10 to 12 minutes. Taste and add more salt to your liking.

4. To make the tacos, heat a medium skillet or comal over high heat. Add a tortilla and cook for 30 to 40 seconds on each side, then transfer to a tortilla holder or wrap in a kitchen towel. Repeat to heat the remaining tortillas.

5. Add 2 tablespoons of the picadillo mixture to one half of each tortilla and fold to close. They should stay closed as you fry them, but feel free to use toothpicks if necessary.

6. Heat the oil in a large, deep sauté pan over medium heat. Working in batches, add a few tacos and fry for 2 minutes on each side, or until golden brown. Using a spatula, transfer the tacos to a paper towel–lined plate.

7. Serve with salsa.

GRINGA AL PASTOR TACOS

MAKES 8 TACOS

TVP:

1 (8-ounce) package TVP strips, such as Butler Soy Curls

SAUCE:

2 tablespoons neutral oil, such as avocado oil, divided

½ medium white onion, thinly sliced

7 whole black peppercorns

2 whole cloves

3 garlic cloves, minced

6 guajillo chiles, stemmed and seeded

1½ cups low-sodium vegetable broth

2 bay leaves

1 tablespoon dried oregano

½ teaspoon ground cumin

¼ teaspoon ground allspice

2 to 6 canned chipotle peppers in adobo

1 cup large pineapple chunks (from about ⅓ pineapple), divided

1½ tablespoons apple cider vinegar

¾ teaspoon sea salt

(Continued)

Tacos al pastor served in corn tortillas are great. Tacos al pastor served between two lightly pan-fried flour tortillas with melty cheese and caramelized onions are *divine*. Al pastor tacos are a classic and common street taco in Mexico, usually containing a protein slow-cooked with pineapple and onion. On a recent trip to Mexico City, my husband and I ordered vegan al pastor tacos from a street stand; I ordered the classic taco with corn tortilla, and when my husband learned "gringa style" meant it was served between two flour tortillas with melty cheese, he didn't hesitate. A bit jealous, I ended up convincing him to trade me one of my corn tortilla tacos for his delicious gringa al pastor taco because they looked to die for. Eso si es amor! *Now that's love!* For this recipe I love using TVP, which can be found at nearly all Mexican grocery stores and online.

---

1. Put the TVP in a large bowl and cover with hot water. Place a bowl or plate on top so that the TVP is fully submerged. Soak for 20 minutes. Drain in a colander, then squeeze the TVP to release more water. Return the TVP to the bowl.

2. To make the sauce, heat the oil in a large, deep sauté pan over medium heat. Add the onion and sauté for 2 to 3 minutes. Add the peppercorns and cloves and cook for 2 minutes, then turn the heat down to low, add the garlic, and sauté for 2 minutes. Add the guajillo chiles and cook for 1 minute, stirring continuously. Add the broth, bay leaves, oregano, cumin, and allspice, turn the heat up to medium, and simmer for 8 minutes.

3. Remove the bay leaves and carefully transfer the contents of the pan to a blender. Add the chipotle peppers, half of the pineapple chunks, the vinegar, and salt. Blend on high until smooth. If the blender is sticking, add another ¼ cup broth.

4. Pour the contents of the blender over the TVP and mix well. Add the remaining pineapple chunks and make sure they're coated in the sauce as well. Cover with plastic wrap and let sit at room temperature for 20 minutes or in the fridge overnight for even better flavor.

5. To make the tacos, heat 1 tablespoon oil in a large skillet over medium-low heat. Add the onion and cook for 2 minutes, then add about a third of the TVP mixture, doing your best to leave the marinade and pineapple

(Continued)

(Continued)

TACOS:

3 tablespoons neutral high-heat oil, such as avocado oil, divided

¼ medium white onion, thinly sliced

Sea salt

8 flour tortillas, store-bought or homemade (page 30)

1 (8-ounce) package shredded plant-based mozzarella cheese

2 avocados, halved, pitted, peeled, and sliced

¼ bunch cilantro, finely chopped

2 limes, cut into wedges

¼ white onion, finely diced

chunks behind. Cook for 2 to 3 minutes, then stir and cook for another 2 to 3 minutes. Repeat this process 5 or 6 times, until the TVP begins to char. Season with a pinch of salt. Transfer to a bowl. Repeat to cook the remaining 2 batches of TVP, using 1 tablespoon oil for each batch. Once the last batch is cooked, return everything to the pan, reserving the pineapple in the marinade. Turn the heat down to low and cook for 10 minutes. Transfer to a large bowl.

6. Using a slotted spoon, transfer the pineapple chunks from the marinade to the same pan. Cook over medium-high heat for 2 minutes on each side, or until charred. Transfer to a cutting board and cut into small pieces.

7. Heat a large skillet or comal over medium heat. Add a flour tortilla. Sprinkle ¼ cup shredded cheese on one half of the tortilla and fold over, like a quesadilla. Cook for 1 to 2 minutes on each side, until the cheese is melted. Open the tortilla and add about 2 tablespoons of the TVP mixture, top with sliced avocado, chopped cilantro, a squeeze of lime juice, diced onion, and a small piece or two of pineapple. Press the tortilla closed. Repeat to make the remaining tacos.

❖ BAJA PALMITOS TACOS ❖

Baja Hearts of Palm "Fish" Tacos

MAKES 8 TO 10 TACOS

"FISH":

1 (14-ounce) can hearts of palm, drained

½ teaspoon celery salt or sea salt

1 large sheet nori (optional)

BEER BATTER:

1 cup all-purpose flour or gluten-free baking blend (such as Bob's Red Mill Gluten-Free 1-to-1 Baking Flour)

2 tablespoons cornstarch

1 tablespoon paprika

1 teaspoon baking powder

1 teaspoon garlic powder

1 teaspoon onion powder

½ teaspoon sea salt

½ teaspoon ground black pepper

1 cup light beer or sparkling water

TACOS:

12 cups neutral oil, such as avocado oil

8 to 10 corn or flour tortillas, store-bought or homemade (pages 34 and 30)

If there is a Baja fish taco on the menu, no questions asked, I order it. This was true for both my pre-vegan days and now when I am at a vegan restaurant. There is something irresistible about that crispy fried batter and tender, flaky inside! These tacos transport me back to the many fish tacos my husband and I ate in our college days from the $1 taco truck in our hometown. Growing up 15 minutes from Baja California, I have had my share of delicious beer-battered fish tacos and felt fairly equipped when setting out to create a vegan version. The use of hearts of palm will surprise you! They have a flaky, tender texture, very similar to that of white fish, and with the help of nori (a type of seaweed), we get a beautiful seafood flavor that makes these tacos crave-worthy for vegans and nonvegans alike! That said, you can leave out the nori if you can't find it or don't like it. These tacos are best enjoyed beachside with a crisp chilled beer in hand, but even if you're far from a shore, they will make you feel like you've got your feet in the sand.

---

1. To make the "fish," put the hearts of palm on a cutting board and pat dry with a paper towel. With the bottom of a plate, press down on each heart of palm to flatten it while still keeping it intact. Season with the celery salt.

2. Using kitchen scissors, cut a piece of nori (if using) the size of each heart of palm and place on top of each flattened piece (it should adhere to the moisture). Cover with plastic wrap and then place a plate face-down on top. Let sit for 5 minutes while you make the batter.

3. In a large bowl, combine the flour, cornstarch, paprika, baking powder, garlic powder, onion powder, salt, and pepper and mix well. Pour in the beer and whisk until smooth.

4. To make the tacos, heat the oil in a large pot over medium heat until it reaches 350°F; if you don't have a thermometer, you can drop about ½ teaspoon batter into the oil to test readiness. It should become a golden piece of fried dough in 50 to 60 seconds.

(Continued)

(Continued)

TO SERVE:

⅓ cup Mayonesa de Limón (page 36) mixed with 2 tablespoons plain, unsweetened plant-based milk *or* ⅓ cup store-bought vegan mayonnaise mixed with 2 tablespoons fresh lime juice

½ head green cabbage, cored and shredded or thinly sliced

¼ onion, finely diced

¼ bunch cilantro, chopped

Salsa de Mango (page 83) or Abuelita's Salsa de Piña y Habanero (page 91)

2 or 3 limes, cut into wedges

5. Add one heart of palm to the batter. Coat evenly, then use two forks to carefully lift it from the batter and transfer to the hot oil. Cook until golden brown on both sides, 2 to 3 minutes total. Use a spider to transfer to a paper towel–lined plate. Cut into the "fish" to make sure the center is hot and steamy. If it is hot, continue to batter and fry the hearts of palm, cooking up to 4 pieces at a time. If not, return the piece to the oil for another minute or so, and increase the heat slightly for the remaining pieces.

6. Heat a large skillet or comal over high heat. Add a tortilla and cook for 30 to 40 seconds on each side. Repeat to heat the remaining tortillas. To each tortilla, add a piece of "fish," drizzle with the mayo mixture, and top with shredded cabbage, diced onion, cilantro, salsa, and an extra squeeze of lime.

TACOS DE BARBACOA

MAKES 9 TO 12 TACOS

SAUCE:

6 guajillo chiles, stemmed and seeded

4 California chiles, stemmed and seeded

2 pasilla chiles, stemmed and seeded

2 bay leaves

½ (12-ounce) can light beer (such as Corona Light) or sparkling water

¼ cup white wine vinegar or apple cider vinegar

6 garlic cloves, peeled

1 tablespoon dried oregano

1½ teaspoons fresh or dried thyme

4 whole cloves

Sea salt

3 tablespoons neutral oil, such as avocado oil

TACOS:

1½ pounds Yukon Gold potatoes, peeled and cut into quarters

4 tablespoons neutral oil, such as avocado oil, divided

1 pound oyster or king oyster mushrooms, thinly sliced or shredded with a fork

Sea salt

7 tablespoons neutral oil, such as avocado oil, divided

My Grandma Esther's barbacoa was something we eagerly awaited every Nochebuena (Christmas Eve). My grandmother was a lover of traditions and I adored that about her. We knew what to expect—and look forward to—every Christmas spent with her. The table would be elegantly set, our seats would be assigned with little name tags with her perfect cursive handwriting, and Luis Miguel's Christmas album would be playing on her 1980s CD player.

My grandma would spend days preparing barbacoa using a combination of beef and pork, dried chiles, herbs, and vinegar, slow cooked until tender. Barbacoa means more than just the taste and deliciousness: it's the memories and loving energy attached to it. I used my grandmother's marinade recipe, including three different types of dried chiles, to make this delicious mushroom version and made sure to add her secret ingredient: potatoes. These tacos are delicious with a side of Abuelita's Arroz Blanco (page 41) or Arroz Rojo (page 44). *Note: In this recipe, we want true pasilla chiles, which are dried chilaca peppers.*

1. To make the sauce, put the dried chiles and bay leaves in a large pot, cover with water, and bring to a boil over medium-high heat. Cook for 10 minutes, then drain, reserving 1½ cups of the cooking liquid. Wipe out the pot.

2. Transfer the chiles, bay leaves, and reserved chile cooking liquid to a blender, along with the beer, vinegar, garlic cloves, oregano, thyme, cloves, and a pinch of salt. Blend on high until smooth.

3. Heat the oil in the same pot over medium-low heat. Hold a fine-mesh strainer over the pot and pour the blended mixture through the strainer, then discard the solids in the strainer. Cook the sauce for 15 minutes, stirring continuously.

4. Meanwhile, put the potatoes in a medium pot, cover with water, and bring to a boil over high heat. Cook for 17 to 20 minutes, until fork-tender, then drain.

5. Heat 2 tablespoons oil in a large sauté pan over medium heat. Add about half of the mushrooms and let them cook, undisturbed, for 3 minutes, or until golden, then stir so they cook on the other side for 3 minutes, or until golden all over. Season with a pinch of salt. Transfer

9 to 12 corn or flour tortillas, store-bought or homemade (pages 34 and 30)

2 avocados, halved, pitted, peeled, and sliced

the mushrooms to a paper towel–lined plate. Cook the remaining mushrooms in the same away, using the remaining 2 tablespoons oil and another pinch of salt. Return the first batch of mushrooms to the pan, then add the blended sauce and the potatoes. Mix to combine, turn the heat down to low, and cook for 10 minutes. Taste and add salt to your liking.

6. Heat a large skillet or comal over high heat. Add a tortilla and cook for 30 to 40 seconds on each side. Repeat to heat the remaining tortillas. Spoon some of the barbacoa mixture on each tortilla, then top with avocado.

TACOS DE "CHICHARRÓN" DE SETAS EN SALSA VERDE

Oyster Mushroom "Chicharrón" Tacos in Green Salsa

MAKES 8 TACOS

½ cup cornstarch

1 teaspoon onion powder

½ teaspoon garlic powder

½ teaspoon chili powder

¼ teaspoon ground cumin

¼ teaspoon sea salt

1 pound oyster mushrooms

⅓ cup + 2 tablespoons neutral high-heat oil, such as avocado oil, divided

1 medium white onion, thinly sliced

2 cups Salsa Verde (page 81)

8 corn or flour tortillas, store-bought or homemade (pages 34 and 30)

TO SERVE (OPTIONAL):

½ bunch cilantro, chopped

1 or 2 avocados, halved, pitted, peeled, and sliced

2 limes, cut into wedges

The first time I made them, these "chicharrón" tacos made my eyes widen and hips move with joy with every bite I took. Pan-fried to a golden crisp on the outside, soft and meaty on the inside—they're simply delectable. While traditional chicharrón can be thought of as an indulgence, as it's made of fried pork skin, this oyster mushroom iteration offers a slightly healthier version with all of the flavor. Oyster mushrooms have a uniquely meaty texture and, when fried with a little cornstarch, become crispy, golden gems of tender, plant-based "chicharrón." The brightness of the salsa verde here pairs wonderfully with the richness of the fried mushrooms, making these tacos feel like a special indulgence for meat eaters and vegetable lovers alike!

---

1. In a medium bowl, combine the cornstarch, onion powder, garlic powder, chili powder, cumin, and salt and mix well.

2. Using your hands, break apart the oyster mushrooms into either individual mushrooms or, if they are on the small side, into clusters of 2 or 3 mushrooms. Working in 2 or 3 batches, thoroughly coat the mushrooms in the cornstarch mixture, then set aside on a plate.

3. Heat ⅓ cup oil in a large, deep sauté pan over medium heat. After 2 or 3 minutes, add 1 coated mushroom to the oil: if it sizzles, the oil is hot enough; if not, let it heat a bit longer. Working in batches and adding only as many mushrooms as will fit while leaving 1 inch between them, fry for 2 to 3 minutes on each side, until golden, flipping with a fork or kitchen tongs. Transfer the golden, crispy mushrooms to a paper towel–lined plate and lightly sprinkle with salt.

4. Wipe out the pan and heat the remaining 2 tablespoons oil over medium-low heat. Add the onion and sauté for 3 minutes. Add the salsa verde and simmer for 5 minutes. Add the crispy fried mushrooms and mix well.

5. Heat a comal or large skillet over high heat. Add a tortilla and cook for 30 to 40 seconds on each side. Repeat to heat the remaining tortillas. Add a spoonful of the fried mushroom mixture to each tortilla, then enjoy as is or top with cilantro, avocado, and a squeeze of fresh lime juice.

TACOS DORADOS DE PAPA

Crispy Potato Tacos

MAKES 12 TACOS

2½ pounds Yukon Gold potatoes, peeled and chopped into small 1-inch cubes

2 tablespoons sea salt, divided

¼ cup Crema Mexicana (page 37) or store-bought vegan sour cream

2 tablespoons vegan butter

1 teaspoon garlic powder

¼ teaspoon ground black pepper

12 corn or flour tortillas, store-bought or homemade (pages 34 and 30)

6 tablespoons neutral oil, such as avocado oil

TO SERVE:

½ head iceberg lettuce, cored and shredded

Crema Mexicana (page 37) or store-bought vegan sour cream

Salsa Verde (page 81)

¼ bunch cilantro, chopped

¼ small white or red onion, diced very small

My Grandma Esther loved her taquitos de papa, filled with creamy, crispy mashed potato, and each time I make them for an easy comfort meal, I feel her sweet soul with me. I have a clear image in my mind of seeing the joy on my grandmother's face as she ate her tacos with a mound of lettuce on top and a generous spoonful of salsa verde for each bite. The last few years of my grandmother's life, she spent less time in the kitchen due to an illness, and although the tacos de papa came from a local shop rather than her kitchen, they still brought her so much joy. I could see that it lit up her inner child and brought her comfort, and that's what I hope these homemade ones do for you as well. The potato filling is creamy and has a subtle buttery flavor thanks to the use of vegan butter. These pair well with salsa verde and crema, but you could also serve them with Salsa de Calabacita Taquera (page 87).

---

1. Put the potatoes in a large pot, cover with water, and add 1½ tablespoons salt. Bring to a boil over high heat and cook for 15 to 17 minutes, until fork-tender. Drain and transfer to a large bowl.

2. Using a large fork or potato masher, mash the potatoes, then add the crema, butter, garlic powder, remaining ½ tablespoon salt, and pepper and mix well. The consistency should be smooth but with small chunks of potato. Taste and add more salt if needed.

3. Heat a large skillet or comal over high heat. Add a tortilla and heat for 30 to 40 seconds on each side, then transfer to a tortilla holder or wrap in a kitchen towel. Repeat to heat the remaining tortillas.

4. Add 2 generous tablespoons of the potato filling to one half of each tortilla and fold to close. Leave a border of tortilla around the edge of the filling so the potato mixture isn't too close to the edge or spilling out. They should stay closed as you fry them, but feel free to use toothpicks if necessary.

5. Heat the oil in a large, deep sauté pan over medium-low heat. Working in batches, add a few potato tacos and fry for 2 minutes on each side, or until golden. Using a spatula, transfer the crispy tacos to a paper towel–lined plate.

6. Serve with shredded lettuce, crema, salsa, cilantro, and diced onion.

TAQUITOS DE FLOR DE JAMAICA

Hibiscus Flower Rolled Tacos

MAKES 8 TO 10 ROLLED TACOS

HIBISCUS FLOWERS:

1 cup dried hibiscus flowers

5 cups water

2 cups low-sodium vegetable broth

SAUCE:

4 tablespoons neutral oil, such as avocado oil, divided

¾ medium white or yellow onion, ½ roughly chopped and ¼ thinly sliced

3 garlic cloves, peeled

1 serrano pepper, stemmed

3 ripe Roma tomatoes

2 guajillo chiles, stemmed and seeded

½ cup low-sodium vegetable broth

¼ cup roasted peanuts

¼ teaspoon sea salt

Ground black pepper

TAQUITOS:

8 to 10 corn or flour tortillas, store-bought or homemade (pages 34 and 30)

⅓ cup neutral high-heat oil, such as avocado oil

TO SERVE:

½ head iceberg lettuce, shredded

¼ medium white or yellow onion, finely diced

Mexican cooking is incredibly resourceful and often centers on a goal of minimizing waste. This dish is a great example of that goal of zero waste, with the hibiscus flowers being used as a taco filling while also creating delicious agua de jamaica as a by-product! Flor de jamaica (dried hibiscus flowers) makes for a tasty taquito or taco filling, providing a slightly chewy, shredded beef–like texture (without any flowery flavor) when they're prepared with extra love and intention.

---

1. In a large pot, combine the hibiscus flowers and water. Bring to a boil over medium-high heat and boil for 10 minutes. Drain the hibiscus flowers, reserving the cooking liquid. Transfer the liquid to a pitcher and add sugar to your liking or keep unsweetened. You now have agua de jamaica, which you can enjoy over ice! Return the hibiscus flowers to the pot, add the broth, and bring to a boil over medium-high heat. Boil for 15 minutes, or until most of the broth has evaporated.

2. Meanwhile, make the sauce. Heat 2 tablespoons oil in a large sauté pan or skillet over medium heat. Add the roughly chopped onion, garlic cloves, serrano pepper, and whole tomatoes. Sauté for 4 to 6 minutes, until the vegetables are slightly charred. Transfer the contents of the pan to a blender. Add the guajillo chiles to the same pan and cook over medium heat for 15 seconds on each side, then add to the blender. Add the broth, peanuts, and salt to the blender and blend on high for 1 minute, or until smooth.

3. Drain the hibiscus flowers in the sink and rinse under cool running water, then put them in the center of a thin kitchen towel or in a nut milk bag and form into a bundle. Squeeze to press out all the liquid. Transfer the hibiscus flowers to a cutting board and chop as finely as possible.

4. Heat the remaining 2 tablespoons oil in a large sauté pan over medium heat. Add the thinly sliced onion and sauté for 2 minutes. Add the hibiscus flowers and sauté for 4 to 5 minutes. Season with a pinch of salt and pepper, then pour in enough of the blended sauce to cover the hibiscus. Turn the heat down to low and cook for 8 to 10 minutes, until the sauce thickens.

5. To make the taquitos, heat a comal or medium skillet over high heat. Add a tortilla and heat for 30 to 40 seconds, then transfer to a tortilla holder or wrap in a kitchen towel. Repeat to heat the remaining tortillas.

2 avocados, halved, pitted, peeled, and sliced

¼ bunch cilantro, finely chopped

2 limes, cut into wedges

Crema Mexicana (page 37) or store-bought vegan sour cream

6. Add 2 spoonfuls of the hibiscus mixture to one half of each tortilla, then roll up tightly to form a cigar shape.

7. Heat the oil in a large, deep sauté pan over medium heat. Working in batches, add the taquitos to the oil, seam side down, and fry for 2 to 3 minutes on each side, until golden. Using tongs, transfer the taquitos to a paper towel–lined plate.

8. Top the taquitos with lettuce, onion, avocado, cilantro, a squeeze of fresh lime juice, and crema.

TACOS DE "CARNITAS"

MAKES 10 TACOS

2 (20-ounce) cans green jackfruit in brine, drained and rinsed

¾ medium white onion, thinly sliced, divided

4 garlic cloves, peeled, 2 left whole and 2 minced

6 tablespoons neutral oil, such as avocado oil, divided

1 pound oyster or king oyster mushrooms, thinly sliced or shredded with a fork

½ teaspoon sea salt, divided

1 cup low-sodium vegetable broth

¼ cup fresh orange juice

¼ cup plain, unsweetened plant-based milk

5 thyme sprigs

2 bay leaves

1½ teaspoons brown sugar

2 tablespoons lime juice

10 corn tortillas, store-bought or homemade (page 34)

TO SERVE:

2 avocados, halved, pitted, peeled, and sliced

¼ medium white onion, finely diced

¼ bunch cilantro, chopped

2 or 3 limes, cut into wedges

Carnitas translates to "little meats" in English, and as the Mexican version of pulled pork, it usually offers a delicate, melt-in-your-mouth texture and experience. It was not a meal we often enjoyed at home because of its indulgent nature, but instead was something I would look forward to as a treat at family parties or special occasions. The combination of jackfruit and oyster mushrooms makes for the perfect vegan carnitas: the jackfruit brings the texture, and the mushrooms provide a savory, rich umami flavor. I call for oyster mushrooms here, but you can also use lion's mane or cremini mushrooms. This recipe will take love, care, and a little patience, but I promise it's totally worth it. Might as well put on some Luis Miguel while you're cooking!

---

1. Put the jackfruit in a large bowl and remove the soft seed inside each piece. Transfer the jackfruit to a medium pot. Cover with water (about 5 inches above the jackfruit) and add one-quarter of the sliced onion and the whole garlic cloves. Bring to a boil over medium heat and cook for 15 minutes. Drain, set aside the onion and garlic, and rinse the jackfruit under cool running water. Put the jackfruit in the center of a thin kitchen towel or in a nut milk bag and form into a bundle. Squeeze to press out all the liquid. Transfer the jackfruit, onion, and garlic to a cutting board and roughly chop.

2. Meanwhile, heat 1 tablespoon oil in a large, deep sauté pan over medium-low heat. Add the remaining sliced onion and sauté for 3 minutes. Move the onion to the edges of the pan and add another 2 tablespoons oil. Add the mushrooms and sauté for 7 to 10 minutes, until golden, slowly working in the onion and seasoning with ¼ teaspoon salt. Transfer to a plate.

3. Add the remaining 3 tablespoons oil to the same pan, still over medium-low heat. Add the jackfruit and cook, undisturbed, for 2 to 4 minutes, until golden on one side, then stir to allow the other side to become golden and crisp for 2 to 4 minutes. Season with the remaining ¼ teaspoon salt. Return the mushroom mixture to the pan, add the minced garlic, and mix well. Add the broth, orange juice, milk, thyme sprigs, bay leaves, and brown sugar, turn the heat up to medium, and cook, stirring occasionally, until the liquid is absorbed, 25 to 30 minutes. Remove bay leaves and thyme and stir in the lime juice. Taste and adjust the salt to your liking.

4. Heat a large skillet or comal over high heat. Add a tortilla and heat for 30 to 40 seconds on each side. Repeat to heat the remaining tortillas. To each tortilla, add a couple spoonfuls of then top with avocado slices, diced onion, cilantro, and a squeeze of fresh lime juice.

Mole

An Introduction to Mole

The dish that most represents the heart and soul of Mexican cuisine is mole (pronounced MOH-lay). A unique experience of endlessly flavorful layers, consisting of chiles, nuts, seeds, spices, herbs, dried fruits, chocolate, and tomatoes, mole is a sweet, spicy, savory, smoky, and luscious sauce that is often made for celebrations, from baptisms to weddings.

Unlike quite anything else, mole is a special dish whose roots lie in the pre-Hispanic cooking techniques of the country's Indigenous people. The original ingredients of a mole were dictated by what was available to them, but usually included cacao, tomatoes, pumpkin seeds, and chiles. As the Spanish arrived, the ingredients they brought with them were slowly incorporated into the tradition as well, leading to the array of varieties that exist today.

The two main regions in Mexico known for mole are Puebla and Oaxaca. Puebla's traditional mole is mole poblano (which can contain up to 30 ingredients and tends to be on the sweeter side), while Oaxaca is known for its seven different varieties that trend a bit spicier: negro, rojo, amarillo, verde, coloradito, estofado, and chichilo. Beyond that, every family's recipe for mole, whether mole negro or mole rojo, is different, unique, and a source of pride. Harking back to Mexican culinary traditions of cooking with local ingredients and whatever is in season, each mole is defined by the ingredients, measurements, and techniques unique to the chef or home cook making it. This dish is so much a part of Mexicanness that the creation of a mole can lean more toward a *feeling* verses preciseness in measurements or ingredients. A dish that takes time, intention, and your full presence, mole is a true celebration of Mexican culture, from its indigenous roots to modern cuisine.

MOLE NEGRO CON SETAS ASADAS

Black Mole with Roasted Oyster Mushrooms

SERVES 6

MOLE:

2 cups low-sodium vegetable broth

6 tablespoons neutral oil, such as avocado oil, divided

4 puya chiles, stemmed and seeded

3 guajillo chiles, stemmed and seeded

3 ancho chiles, stemmed and seeded

¼ teaspoon coriander seeds

¼ cup sesame seeds

¼ cup pumpkin seeds

3 whole cloves

1 cinnamon stick

½ star anise

½ Bolillo roll (page 52) *or* 1 (4-inch) piece French bread, cut into 4 pieces

½ medium yellow onion, quartered

1 ripe Roma tomato, halved

3 garlic cloves, peeled

¼ cup raisins

¼ cup cane sugar

1 (3.3-ounce) disk Mexican chocolate (such as Ibarra), roughly chopped

1 teaspoon sea salt

Of all the versions of mole out there, my favorites tend to be iterations on mole negro, for its perfect balance of subtle spice, sweetness, nuttiness, and endless layers of flavor. I found this recipe in the recipe box my Tía Cristy passed down to the family, and it was the very first mole I made from scratch. I initially felt intimidated by the idea of mole as I stared at the long list of ingredients written out by my tía on an old piece of paper. I quickly realized that while making mole does take time, it is actually quite straightforward and, beyond that, incredibly rewarding. I will never forget the overwhelming feeling when tasting my first spoonful of the mole I spent hours on: a combination of joy, pride, and a beautiful, deep connection to my roots. Making mole is a true act of love. To me, my family, and my people, cooking is not only a means to an end of feeding oneself, it's also an art form, and a way of showing love for our family and our culture. As such, there is no rushing involved; it is an opportunity to be present and intentional. Mole negro, which gets its dark color and sweet flavor profile from chocolate, is typically served over chicken, but this mole can be used in whatever way you want. My favorite plating is with roasted oyster mushrooms and a side of homemade tortillas, in Enmoladas de Platano Macho (page 199). *Note: The flavors of the mole develop as they sit, and this sauce will taste even better after 1 to 3 days in the fridge.*

---

1. To make the mole, heat the broth in the microwave or on the stovetop until hot.

2. Heat 2 tablespoons oil in a large sauté pan over medium heat. Add the chiles and cook for 10 seconds on each side, or until lightly charred (watch closely as they will char quickly). Transfer the chiles to a blender, add the hot broth, and let the chiles soak while you toast the remaining ingredients.

3. Add the coriander seeds to the same pan and toast over medium heat for 5 seconds, then transfer to the blender.

4. Add the sesame seeds, pumpkin seeds, cloves, cinnamon stick, and star anise to the pan and toast over medium heat, stirring continuously, for 1 to 2 minutes, until golden. Transfer to the blender.

(Continued)

(Continued)

OYSTER MUSHROOMS:

3 tablespoons neutral oil, such as avocado oil, or extra-virgin olive oil

1 tablespoon fresh or dried oregano

½ teaspoon garlic powder

½ teaspoon sea salt

¼ teaspoon ground black pepper

1½ pounds king oyster mushrooms

TO SERVE:

¼ cup sesame seeds

Corn tortillas, store-bought or homemade (page 34), warmed

5. Turn the heat down to medium-low. Add 2 tablespoons oil to the pan and, when hot, add the bread pieces and toast on each side for 1 minute, or until golden. Transfer to the blender.

6. Add the onion and tomato to the pan and cook over medium-low heat, undisturbed, for 4 minutes, then flip and cook for an additional 4 minutes, until beginning to char. Add the garlic cloves and cook for 2 minutes on each side, or until slightly charred. Transfer to the blender. Remove the pan from the heat.

7. Add the raisins, sugar, chocolate, and salt to the blender and blend on high until smooth, 1 to 2 minutes.

8. Heat the remaining 2 tablespoons oil in a large, deep sauté pan over medium-low heat. Hold a fine-mesh strainer over the pan and pour the contents of the blender through the strainer, then discard the solids in the strainer. The sauce should be smooth and creamy, with a consistency similar to Alfredo sauce. If it is too thick, stir in another ¼ to ½ cup broth or water. Taste and add more salt to your liking. Turn the heat down to low, partially cover the pan, and cook, stirring occasionally, for 25 to 30 minutes. Since the mole is fairly thick, it will not come to a simmer.

9. Meanwhile, preheat the oven to 400°F for the mushrooms.

10. In a small bowl, combine the oil, oregano, garlic powder, salt, and pepper and mix well.

11. Lay the whole oyster mushrooms on a rimmed baking sheet and evenly drizzle the oil mixture over the mushrooms, then gently toss with your hands, making sure everything is well coated. Roast for 12 minutes, then flip the mushrooms and roast for an additional 12 minutes, or until golden and crispy.

12. To serve, add a generous spoonful of mole to each plate, then top with some of the crispy golden mushrooms, garnish with sesame seeds, and enjoy with warm tortillas.

MOLE VERDE CON TOFU EMPANIZADO CON TOTOPOS

Green Mole with Tortilla-Crusted Tofu

SERVES 6

MOLE:

1 pound tomatillos, husked

2 poblano peppers (sometimes labeled pasilla peppers), stemmed and seeded

1 or 2 serrano peppers, stemmed

½ bunch cilantro

½ cup sesame seeds

½ cup pumpkin seeds

1 small white onion, roughly chopped

4 romaine lettuce leaves

3 garlic cloves, peeled

1 tablespoon dried epazote *or* 2 epazote sprigs (optional)

½ teaspoon sea salt

3½ cups low-sodium vegetable broth

5 tablespoons neutral oil, such as avocado oil

CRISPY TORTILLA-CRUSTED TOFU:

3 cups tortilla chips

1 teaspoon dried oregano

¼ teaspoon ground cumin

¼ cup plain, unsweetened plant-based milk

1 (14- to 16-ounce) package firm tofu

¼ teaspoon sea salt

The credit for this mole verde recipe goes to my dad's cousin Betha, who I didn't get the pleasure of knowing but was said to be an incredible cook. I believe it to my core because this recipe truly blew my mind, and I know it will do the same for you. Mole verde is typically a lighter mole with herbaceous notes, ideal for pairing with a crunchy tofu steak.

The ingredient list is much shorter than many mole recipes, and the majority of the ingredients go in raw (eliminating the roasting step), making it a great weekday recipe that nevertheless feels celebratory. While this mole is traditionally served with chicken, I took inspiration from my wedding menu: we had the honor of having our wedding catered by an outstanding Oaxacan chef in Mérida, Mexico, in 2022. She used very innovative techniques to create traditional Mexican recipes with vegan ingredients, and the main course included a tofu steak that was breaded with crushed tortillas instead of bread crumbs. When I was testing this recipe, I found that a mole verde pairs well with the crispy, earthy, and nutty tortilla-crusted tofu. *Note: The flavors of the mole develop as they sit, and this sauce will taste even better after 1 to 3 days in the fridge.*

---

1. Combine all the mole ingredients except the oil in a blender and blend on high until smooth. If you have a small blender, you can do the blending in batches.

2. Heat the oil in a large pot over medium heat. Pour the blended mixture into the pot and cook for 10 minutes, then turn the heat down to low and cook for 45 minutes. The sauce should thicken as it cooks. Taste and add more salt if needed.

3. Meanwhile, make the tortilla-crusted tofu. In a food processor or blender, combine the tortilla chips, oregano, and cumin and pulse until you reach a bread crumb texture. Transfer the mixture to a medium bowl and set aside.

4. Pour the milk into a small bowl and set aside.

(Continued)

(Continued)

⅛ teaspoon ground black pepper

6 tablespoons neutral high-heat oil, such as avocado oil

TO SERVE:

¼ cup sesame seeds

¼ small white onion, very thinly sliced

Corn tortillas, store-bought or homemade (page 34), warmed

5. Wrap the tofu in a kitchen towel or paper towel and gently squeeze for 10 to 15 seconds to remove the excess water. Cut the block of tofu crosswise into ¼-inch-thick slabs. Season with the salt and pepper. Set the tofu, milk, and tortilla crumbs in a row to make your dredging station.

6. Heat the oil in a large skillet over medium heat. Dip a piece of tofu into the milk, then dredge it in the tortilla crumbs, coating both sides. Add the tofu to the hot oil and cook for 2 minutes on each side, until golden, flipping with tongs. Transfer to a paper towel–lined plate and immediately sprinkle with salt. Repeat with the remaining tofu.

7. To serve, add a generous spoonful of mole to each plate, top with a piece of crispy tofu, garnish with sesame seeds and sliced onion, and enjoy with warm tortillas.

MOLE ROJO CON COLIFLOR ASADA

Red Mole with Roasted Cauliflower

SERVES 8

MOLE:

6 cups low-sodium vegetable broth

7 tablespoons neutral oil, such as avocado oil, divided

6 ancho chiles, stemmed and seeded

6 mulato chiles, stemmed and seeded

6 guajillo chiles, stemmed and seeded

7 chiles de árbol, stemmed and seeded

1-inch piece fresh ginger, peeled

¼ cup sesame seeds

¼ cup pumpkin seeds

¼ cup peanuts

¼ cup pecans

2 corn tortillas, store-bought or homemade (page 34), torn in half

1 medium white onion, roughly chopped

1 large ripe Roma tomato, quartered

3 tomatillos, husked

1 green plantain, peeled and cut into 4 pieces

2 garlic cloves, peeled

½ cinnamon stick, broken into pieces

6 whole black peppercorns

½ (3.3-ounce) disk Mexican chocolate (such as Ibarra), roughly chopped

1 teaspoon sea salt

Mole rojo is a spicy, earthy mole with great depth of flavor and a subtle touch of sweetness. A family friend graciously shared her beloved family recipe with me. The original recipe I received had large quantities of each ingredient, and because it was my first time taking on this recipe, I wanted to follow the measurements precisely. I ended with enough mole to feed the whole neighborhood! Luckily, that was far from being a problem because, wow, the result was so special. I saved a batch for my friend to taste for a stamp of approval, and as I nervously watched her eat it, I saw her eyes light up and a big smile cross her face as she said it tasted like home. I've decreased the yield of her recipe here. My favorite way to serve mole rojo is with roasted cauliflower, a side of homemade tortillas, and Abuelita's Arroz Blanco (page 41), although using this mole in Enmoladas de Platano Macho (page 199) or in Lasagna de Mole (page 178) would be a divine choice too. *Note: The flavors of the mole develop as they sit, and this sauce will taste even better after 1 to 3 days in the fridge.*

---

1. Heat the broth in the microwave or on the stovetop until hot.

2. Heat 2 tablespoons oil in a large sauté pan over medium heat. Add the chiles and cook for 10 seconds on each side, or until slightly charred (watch closely as they will char quickly). Transfer the chiles to a blender, add 2 cups hot broth, and let the chiles soak while you toast the remaining ingredients.

3. Add the ginger, sesame seeds, pumpkin seeds, peanuts, and pecans to the same pan and toast over medium-low heat, stirring continuously, for 1 to 2 minutes, until just golden. Transfer to a medium bowl.

4. Turn the heat up to medium. Add 1 tablespoon oil to the pan and, when hot, add the torn tortillas and toast for 45 seconds on each side, or until golden. Transfer to the bowl of nuts and seeds.

5. Add 2 additional tablespoons oil to the pan and, when hot, add the onion, tomato, tomatillos, and plantain. Cook for 4 to 6 minutes, until golden, then flip. Add the garlic cloves and cook for 1 minute, then flip and cook on the other side for 1 minutes. Transfer the garlic to the bowl of nuts, seeds, and tortillas. Continue to cook the onion, tomato,

(Continued)

(Continued)

ROASTED CAULIFLOWER:

1 head cauliflower, cored and cut into florets

5 tablespoons olive oil

½ teaspoon ground cumin

½ teaspoon garlic powder

½ teaspoon sea salt

¼ teaspoon ground black pepper

TO SERVE:

¼ cup sesame seeds

¼ small white onion, very thinly sliced

Corn tortillas, store-bought or homemade (page 34), warmed

tomatillos, and plantain until golden on the other side, 2 to 3 more minutes. Transfer to the bowl. Remove the pan from the heat.

6. Stir the contents of the bowl so everything is fairly evenly combined. Transfer half of the contents to the blender, along with the cinnamon pieces and peppercorns. Blend on high until super smooth.

7. Heat the remaining 2 tablespoons oil in a large pot over medium heat. Hold a fine-mesh strainer over the pot and pour the contents of the blender through it, then discard the solids in the strainer. Simmer for 5 minutes, then turn the heat down to low.

8. Transfer the remaining ingredients in the bowl to the blender, along with the chocolate, salt, and 3 cups hot broth. Blend on high until smooth. Hold the strainer over the pot and pour the contents of the blender through it, then discard the solids in the strainer. Simmer for 30 to 40 minutes, until smooth and creamy. As it cooks it will thicken; add ½ to 1 cup more broth if it seems to be too thick. Taste and add more salt to your liking.

9. Meanwhile, preheat the oven to 425°F for the cauliflower.

10. Put the cauliflower florets in a baking dish and drizzle with the oil. Sprinkle with the cumin, garlic powder, salt, and pepper and toss well to coat. Roast for 22 minutes, then flip the cauliflower and roast for an additional 5 minutes, or until golden and crispy.

11. To serve, add a generous spoonful of mole to each plate, then top with some roasted cauliflower, garnish with sesame seeds and sliced onion, and enjoy with warm tortillas.

PLATILLOS FUERTES

Main Dishes

TOSTADAS DE CHAMPIÑONES

Mushroom Tostadas

MAKES 10 TOSTADAS

MUSHROOM PICADILLO:

4 tablespoons neutral oil, such as avocado oil, divided

2½ tablespoons vegan butter, divided

½ medium white onion, finely diced

4 garlic cloves, minced

2 pounds cremini mushrooms, finely diced

½ teaspoon sea salt

1½ teaspoons dried oregano

¼ teaspoon ground cumin

TO SERVE:

10 tostadas

2 cups Frijoles Refritos (page 51), warmed

½ head iceberg lettuce, finely shredded

¼ bunch cilantro, chopped

2 avocados, halved, pitted, peeled, and sliced

Crema Mexicana (page 37) or store-bought vegan sour cream

Queso Cotija (page 38) or store-bought vegan feta

Salsa of choice

2 limes, cut into wedges

I have learned a lot of very valuable things from my mom. There are things she told me directly—for example, that I should always stand up for myself when I need to and that showing up as myself in the world is, and will always be, enough. Then there were things she taught me by example: how to be brave and unafraid to take things on independently, how to work hard, and how to do a million and one things at once.

Another important lesson I learned from my mom was that tostadas are the best food for entertaining. It may not seem as significant as the life lessons previously mentioned, but as someone who loves to feed people, it is one I value deeply! You can prepare all the fixings ahead of time, then create a tostada station where everyone can make one to their liking. This takes the pressure off entertaining, and everyone will be satisfied, as tostadas are customizable and an easy win! My mom typically uses shredded chicken for hers, which I swapped for cremini mushrooms for a hearty substitute. *Note: Tostadas can be found next to the tortillas at your grocery store, and either fried or baked will work here.*

---

1. Heat 1 tablespoon oil and ½ tablespoon butter in a large skillet or sauté pan over medium heat. Add the onion and sauté for 3 minutes, then add the garlic and sauté for 2 minutes. Transfer the onion and garlic to a large bowl.

2. Add another ½ tablespoon butter to the same pan. Once melted, add one-quarter of the mushrooms and allow to cook, undisturbed, for 3 to 4 minutes, until golden on one side. Stir, sprinkle lightly with salt, and cook for an additional 3 to 4 minutes. Transfer the mushrooms to the bowl with the onion and garlic. Cook the remaining three batches of mushrooms in the same way, adding another ½ tablespoon butter to the pan each time.

3. Once the last batch is cooked, return all the mushrooms to the pan, along with the onion and garlic. Add the oregano and cumin and mix well. Taste and season with salt to your liking.

4. To each tostada, add a layer of warm beans and a few spoonfuls of mushroom picadillo, then top with shredded lettuce, cilantro, sliced avocado, crema, Cotija cheese, salsa, and a squeeze of lime.

ESPAGUETI VERDE

Poblano–Pumpkin Seed Spaghetti

SERVES 4

¾ cup raw pumpkin seeds

3 poblano peppers (sometimes labeled pasilla peppers)

2 jalapeño peppers

1 tablespoon plus ½ teaspoon sea salt, divided

1 pound spaghetti, bucatini, or other long pasta

3 tablespoons vegan butter or neutral oil, such as avocado oil, divided

½ medium yellow onion, roughly chopped

3 garlic cloves, roughly chopped

1½ cups fresh or frozen corn

⅓ (14-ounce) package medium-firm tofu

¼ bunch cilantro, plus more, chopped, for garnish

1¼ cup plain, unsweetened plant-based milk

¼ teaspoon ground black pepper

2 tablespoons nutritional yeast (optional)

Handful salted cashews (optional)

1 tablespoon high-quality extra-virgin olive oil

In Mexican cooking the goal is often to incorporate heat, smokiness, and creaminess into a dish. Here, we add a Mexican flair to a traditional Italian dish with roasted poblano peppers, onion, garlic, fresh cilantro, and cream blended into a sauce, then tossed with spaghetti. When I set about creating a vegan version of this dish, I looked to history: while a store-bought vegan sour cream or cream cheese would do the trick in replacing the dairy, I chose to tap into an indigenous cooking technique and used pumpkin seeds to add creaminess to the sauce. I also added a touch of tofu for more silkiness and an extra kick of plant protein. This is an easy weeknight dinner or a great meal to take to a family gathering!

---

1. Put the pumpkin seeds in a bowl and cover with boiling water. Set aside to soak while you prepare the remaining ingredients.

2. Roast the poblano and jalapeño peppers on an open flame for 1 to 2 minutes, until charred on all sides. (Alternatively, heat the oven to the highest broiler setting, put the peppers on a rimmed baking sheet lined with aluminum foil, and broil on the middle rack for 1 to 2 minutes on each side, until charred.) Transfer the charred peppers to a bowl, cover with plastic wrap, and let sit for 10 minutes to release steam.

3. Meanwhile, bring a large pot of water to a boil. Add 1 tablespoon salt and the pasta and cook until al dente according to the package instructions. Drain, reserving ½ cup of the pasta cooking water.

4. Melt 1 tablespoon butter in a large sauté pan over medium heat. Add the onion and sauté for 5 minutes, then add the garlic and sauté for 2 minutes. Transfer the onion and garlic to a blender.

5. Add another 1 tablespoon butter to the same pan, still over medium heat, then add the corn and sauté for 4 minutes. Season with ¼ teaspoon salt, then turn off the heat and leave the corn in the pan.

6. Remove the charred skin, stems, inner ribs, and seeds from the peppers. Transfer to the blender with the onion and garlic.

7. Drain the pumpkin seeds. Add the pumpkin seeds to the blender, along with the tofu, cilantro, and milk, and blend on high until smooth.

8. Pour the blended mixture into the pan of corn and cook over medium-low heat for 3 minutes to heat through and thicken, then add the remaining ¼ teaspoon salt and the black pepper. Add the nutritional yeast (if using) and stir to combine.

9. Add the pasta and ¼ to ½ cup reserved pasta cooking water; the sauce should coat the pasta. Stir to combine, then portion into bowls and garnish with chopped cilantro. For a similar taste and feel to parmesan cheese, finely grate a salted cashew over the top of each serving and lightly drizzle with olive oil.

⁂ BIRRIA ⁂

SERVES 6

3 large ripe Roma tomatoes, quartered

1 large or 2 medium carrots, peeled and roughly chopped

6 guajillo chiles, stemmed and seeded

2 ancho chiles, stemmed and seeded

1½ small white onions, ½ left whole, ¾ thinly sliced, and ¼ finely chopped

5 garlic cloves, peeled

2 bay leaves

7 cups low-sodium vegetable broth, divided

1 teaspoon dried oregano

1 teaspoon dried thyme

½ teaspoon ground cinnamon

2 (20-ounce) cans green jackfruit in brine, drained and rinsed

1 cup water

5 tablespoons neutral oil, such as avocado oil, divided

1 teaspoon sea salt, divided

12 ounces king oyster, oyster, or cremini mushrooms, thinly sliced

1 tablespoon cane sugar

1 tablespoon apple cider vinegar

¼ bunch cilantro, chopped

Corn or flour tortillas, store-bought or homemade (pages 34 and 30), warmed

Birria is a rich meat stew that, in recent years, has become very beloved throughout the United States, but its roots go back to colonial Mexico. In the 1600s the Spanish introduced goats to the region as an animal protein, but the tough texture and gamy taste weren't immediately embraced. In typical style, the native people of Jalisco used their innovative cooking skills and distinct spices to create one of the most beloved dishes in Mexican cuisine. The meat was slow-cooked in an underground oven for several hours with various spices and chiles until tender and oh so flavorful, then added to a rich stew.

Today, while birria is still enjoyed in its traditional stew format, its popularity has risen thanks to the creation of the "quesobirria taco," invented in my across-the-border neighbor city, Tijuana. For this dish, a corn or flour tortilla is dipped in the stew, then stuffed with cheese and the birria meat, and finally cooked on a comal until the cheese is melty. It's served with the consomé (broth) for dipping. As this dish evolved, taquerías began using beef, chicken, and other animal proteins in place of goat meat, and in my plant-forward kitchen, I've opted for a combination of mushrooms and jackfruit for a meat-like savory experience that leaves no taste bud unsatisfied.

---

1. In a large pot, combine the tomatoes, carrots, chiles, whole onion piece, 3 garlic cloves, bay leaves, and 4 cups broth. Bring to a boil over high heat and boil for 10 minutes. Add the oregano, thyme, and cinnamon, stir, and continue to boil for another 10 minutes.

2. Meanwhile, put the jackfruit in a large bowl and remove the soft seed inside each piece, then discard. Transfer the jackfruit to a small pot and add the water, 1 cup broth, and remaining 2 garlic cloves. Bring to a boil over high heat and boil for 15 minutes. Drain, discard the garlic cloves, and rinse the jackfruit under cool running water. Put the jackfruit in the center of a thin kitchen towel or in a nut milk bag and form into a bundle. Squeeze to press out all the liquid.

3. Heat 2 tablespoons oil in a large sauté pan or skillet over medium heat. Add the thinly sliced onion and sauté for 2 minutes, then add half of the jackfruit in a single layer. Cook, undisturbed, for 2 to 3 minutes, until beginning to brown. Stir the jackfruit until the other side begins to brown as well, another 2 to 3 minutes. Season with ½ teaspoon salt, then

transfer the jackfruit and onion to a large bowl. Add 1 tablespoon oil to the pan and cook the remaining jackfruit in the same way, then transfer to the bowl.

4. Add 1 tablespoon oil to the pan, still over medium heat, and, when hot, add half of the mushrooms in a single layer. Cook for 4 minutes on each side, or until golden. Transfer the mushrooms to the bowl with the jackfruit. Add the remaining 1 tablespoon oil to the pan and cook the remaining mushrooms in the same way. Once the second batch of mushrooms is cooked, return all the mushrooms and the jackfruit to the pan and stir to combine. Turn the heat down to low.

5. Remove the bay leaves from the large pot of vegetables, then carefully transfer the contents of the pot to a blender, along with the sugar, vinegar, and remaining ½ teaspoon salt. Blend on high for 1 minute. Pour the contents of the blender back into the large pot and bring to a simmer over medium-low heat, then add the remaining 2 cups broth.

6. Pour about ¼ cup of the hot liquid into the pan of mushrooms and jackfruit and stir well, making sure to get any bits stuck to the bottom of the pan. Transfer the contents of the pan to the large pot and stir. Bring to a simmer over medium-low heat and cook for 10 minutes.

7. Ladle the birria into bowls and serve hot, topped with the finely chopped onion and cilantro, with a side of warm tortillas.

REPOLLO ASADO ALMENDRADO

Roasted Cabbage in a Creamy Almond Tomato Sauce

SERVES 4

ROASTED CABBAGE:

1 head cabbage, cut into 1-inch-thick slabs

¼ cup neutral oil, such as avocado oil

½ teaspoon ground cumin

½ teaspoon garlic powder

½ teaspoon sea salt

SAUCE:

4 tablespoons neutral oil, such as avocado oil, divided

3 corn tortillas, store-bought or homemade (page 34), each roughly torn into 3 pieces

4 ripe Roma tomatoes, quartered

½ medium white onion, roughly chopped

2 garlic cloves, peeled

½ cup slivered almonds

2 ancho chiles, stemmed and seeded

1 cup low-sodium vegetable broth

1 teaspoon sea salt

TO SERVE:

¼ cup slivered almonds

2 or 3 cilantro sprigs, chopped

Abuelita's Arroz Blanco (page 41)

Corn or flour tortillas, store-bought or homemade (pages 34 and 30), warmed

A pre-Hispanic culinary technique that the Indigenous people favored was the grinding of nuts and seeds into sauces to create a rich and creamy consistency. Today, many plant-based cooks around the world use this method as well, without realizing that all the credit goes to Indigenous communities such as the Aztecs, who creatively combined ingredients like pumpkin seeds, tomatoes, and chiles to create luscious, flavorful sauces like mole and pipian.

The inspiration for this recipe comes from my abuelita's pollo (chicken) almendrado. I wanted an underdog vegetable to have its moment to shine in place of the chicken, so in comes cabbage. When cut into thick "steaks," dressed up with seasonings and oil, and roasted in the oven, this unsung hero of the vegetable world becomes buttery, slightly sweet, and hearty enough to be a main course dish. *Note: If you would like a replacement that more closely resembles chicken in flavor and texture, I recommend substituting plant-based "chicken" by the brand Daring.*

1. Preheat the oven to 450°F.

2. Spread out the cabbage "steaks" on a rimmed baking sheet, drizzle with the oil, and sprinkle with the cumin, garlic powder, and salt. Rub the cabbage well to evenly coat, then roast for 15 minutes, flip, and continue roasting for another 15 minutes, or until the cabbage is browned and sizzling.

3. Meanwhile, make the sauce. Heat 2 tablespoons oil in a large skillet over medium heat. Add the tortilla pieces, tomatoes, and onion and cook for 7 minutes, flipping the ingredients halfway through. Add the garlic cloves, almonds, and ancho chiles and cook for 30 seconds, stirring continuously. Transfer the ancho chiles to a blender, then continue to cook everything else for 2 minutes on each side, or until golden. Transfer the contents of the pan to the blender, add the broth and salt, and blend on high until smooth.

4. Heat the remaining 2 tablespoons oil in a large, deep sauté pan over medium-low heat. Carefully pour in the blended sauce and simmer for 5 minutes, then turn the heat down to low and cook for 20 minutes. Taste and adjust the salt to your liking.

5. To serve, add a few generous spoonfuls of the sauce to each plate, top with the roasted cabbage, and garnish with slivered almonds and cilantro. Serve with rice and a side of tortillas.

LASAGNA DE MOLE

SERVES 6

4 poblano peppers (sometimes labeled pasilla peppers)

4 tablespoons neutral oil, such as avocado oil, divided

½ medium white onion, thinly sliced

2 garlic cloves, peeled and minced

1½ pounds cremini or king oyster mushrooms, thinly sliced

Sea salt

1 cup fresh or frozen white corn

Mole Negro (page 159—without the roasted mushrooms) *or* 1 (16-ounce) jar black mole paste

1 cup low-sodium vegetable broth, plus 3 additional cups if using jarred mole paste

1 cup tomato sauce

1 (1-pound) package oven-ready lasagna noodles

1 cup Crema Mexicana (page 37) or store-bought vegan sour cream, plus more for serving

1 (8-ounce) package shredded plant-based mozzarella cheese

¼ bunch cilantro, chopped

Lasagna de mole is not traditional in Mexican culture, but it is a tradition in my family after the recipe was handed down to us from a family friend. My mom would make this lasagna for birthdays and special occasions. This dish marries the classic Italian format of lasagna with Mexican ingredients like poblano peppers, corn, crema, and mole layered between the noodles. In place of the chicken that my mom would use in her lasagna, I use mushrooms for a hearty plant-based alternative. The other swaps are quite simple: my cashew-based crema and store-bought shredded vegan cheese make this an easy Sunday night dish you can reheat all week. You are more than welcome to make a mole negro from scratch, but since a lasagna can already be a labor of love, to simplify even further I recommend a mole paste. Doña Maria brand is widely available in most grocery stores, although any mole negro paste will do.

---

1. Roast the poblano peppers on an open flame for 1 to 2 minutes, until charred on all sides. (Alternatively, heat the oven to the highest broiler setting high, put the peppers on a rimmed baking sheet lined with aluminum foil, and broil on the middle oven rack for 1 to 2 minutes on each side, until charred.) Transfer the peppers to a bowl, cover with plastic wrap, and let sit for 10 minutes to release steam.

2. Meanwhile, heat 1 tablespoon oil in a large sauté pan over medium-low heat. Add the onion and sauté for 4 minutes, then add the garlic and sauté for 1 minute. Transfer the onion and garlic to a bowl.

3. Add 1 tablespoon oil to the pan and turn the heat up to medium. Add about a quarter of the mushrooms and cook, undisturbed, for 4 to 5 minutes, until golden brown. Stir and flip to brown the other side for 4 to 5 minutes. Season very lightly with salt. Transfer the mushrooms to the bowl with the onion and garlic. Cook the remaining mushrooms in the same way, adding more oil as needed.

4. Once all the mushrooms are cooked and transferred to the bowl, add the corn to the pan and cook for 5 minutes, seasoning with a pinch of salt. Return the mushrooms, onion, and garlic to the pan and stir to combine. Remove the pan from the heat.

5. Remove the charred skin, stems, inner ribs, and seeds from the poblano peppers. Cut the peppers into thin, 1-inch-long strips. Add the peppers to the mushroom mixture and stir to combine.

6. Preheat the oven to 400°F.

7. Put the mole in a large, deep sauté pan. If using homemade mole, add 1 cup broth; if using jarred mole paste, add 4 cups broth. Add the tomato sauce and stir to combine. Simmer over medium heat for 10 minutes.

8. Coat the bottom of a lasagna pan with ½ cup of the mole mixture and spread evenly, then add a layer of lasagna noodles, followed by a layer of the mushroom mixture, a drizzle of crema, and another layer of the mole mixture. Repeat to make 4 or 5 layers, until all the ingredients are used, then top with the shredded cheese.

9. Cover the lasagna with aluminum foil and bake for 50 minutes. Let it sit, still covered, for 25 minutes before serving. Serve topped with more crema and garnished with the cilantro.

SOPA DE ALBONDIGAS

Mexican Meatball Soup

SERVES 6

SOUP:

8 cups low-sodium vegetable broth

3 ripe Roma tomatoes, roughly chopped

3 canned chipotle peppers in adobo

¼ medium white onion, roughly chopped

2 garlic cloves, peeled

1½ cups water

6 cilantro sprigs

2 large Yukon Gold potatoes, peeled and cut into 1-inch pieces

3 large carrots, peeled and cut into 1-inch pieces

1 zucchini, cut into 1-inch pieces

½ teaspoon sea salt

2 limes, cut into wedges

MEATBALLS:

1 (12-ounce) package plant-based ground meat

½ cup uncooked long-grain white rice

¼ medium yellow or white onion, finely diced

3 garlic cloves, minced

1 ripe Roma tomato, seeded and finely diced

1 tablespoon finely chopped fresh mint

There was a time in my childhood when my dad stepped into the kitchen more as he decided to cook his mother's recipes more consistently for our family. At the time, I didn't have the appreciation I should have had, as I was a teenager. Reflecting now, it really melts my heart to know how much intention and love he put into learning how to make the foods he enjoyed as a child for my siblings and me. Sopa de albondigas was one of his favorites growing up, and as he continued to perfect the recipe over time, it become a favorite of mine as well.

This sopa starts with a light tomato broth with chunky chopped vegetables and herbaceous, flavorful meatballs, served with a spritz of lime juice. It feels like a warm hug in a bowl, and it's a dish I missed deeply when I went vegan. Not just for the flavors and satisfying experience, but also for the love I felt being served a bowl of this sopita by my dad. Feeling nostalgic one cold rainy day, I called my dad for the recipe and substituted a few plant-based ingredients while keeping the foundation of my abuelita's dish true and authentic. The swap for ground beef is easy thanks to the many plant-based ground beef options we have across the United States: the brands Beyond Meat and Impossible are great. Recipes passed down from generation to generation are beautiful and should be treasured, and I will always work hard to recreate them with a plant-based spin to keep traditions alive.

---

1. In a large pot, bring the broth to a boil over high heat.
2. Meanwhile, combine the tomatoes, chipotle peppers, onion, garlic cloves, and water in a blender and blend on high until smooth. Pour the tomato mixture into the boiling broth, add the cilantro, and continue to boil while you make the meatballs.
3. Line a rimmed baking sheet with parchment paper.
4. Combine all of the meatball ingredients in a large bowl and mix well. Lightly coat your hands with oil, then form the meat mixture into about 12 meatballs the size of golf balls. Place them on the prepared baking sheet as you form them.

1 tablespoon dried oregano

½ teaspoon sea salt

⅛ teaspoon ground black pepper

Neutral oil, such as avocado oil, for greasing

2 limes, cut into wedges

5. Add the meatballs to the boiling broth and boil for 15 minutes, then add the potatoes and boil for 5 minutes. Add the carrots and boil for another 5 minutes. Add the zucchini and boil for a final 7 minutes, or until all the vegetables are tender. At this point, you can remove a meatball to test for doneness: the rice should be fully cooked. If not, cook for an additional 5 minutes.

6. Add the salt, then taste the broth and add more if needed. Serve hot with a squeeze of fresh lime.

✵ COLIFLOR ASADA AL PASTOR ✵

Al Pastor Roasted Cauliflower

SERVES 4

CAULIFLOWER:

1 large head cauliflower (or 2 small heads)

1 teaspoon sea salt

2 tablespoons olive oil

MARINADE:

3 tablespoons neutral oil, such as avocado oil

½ small white onion, halved

5 garlic cloves, peeled

7 whole black peppercorns

2 whole cloves

6 guajillo chiles, stemmed and seeded

1 cup low-sodium vegetable broth

2 bay leaves

1 tablespoon dried Mexican oregano or regular oregano

½ teaspoon ground cumin

¼ teaspoon ground allspice

2 to 4 canned chipotle peppers in adobo

4 (1-inch) chunks fresh pineapple, plus ½ cup chopped fresh pineapple

2 tablespoons white wine vinegar or apple cider vinegar

1 teaspoon sea salt

Al pastor was created around the 1920s after a Lebanese immigrant to Mexico introduced the classic shawarma, a popular Middle Eastern dish consisting of thin layers of meat stacked on a vertical rotisserie and slowly roasted. Mexicans adopted the same method of preparing meat, then slowly began to add their own flavors, like spices, chiles, and pineapple, to appeal more to the locals and their palates. The al pastor taco is known for its smoky, spicy, and sweet flavor profile: if you're looking for a plant-based version, see my Gringa al Pastor Tacos (page 141).

The al pastor flavors are too good *not* to use in dishes beyond tacos, especially on cauliflower, with its small crevices that soak up flavor so well. Here, a whole head is bathed in a rich, flavorful marinade, then roasted until slightly charred, for a dish that deserves center place at your next dinner party. This preparation creates a cauliflower that is tender and falls apart like butter, with flavors that will dance around on your taste buds! Serve with Guacasalsa (page 88) and Arroz Verde (page 47). *Note: Mexican oregano has a slightly different flavor profile and is worth using if you can find it in your grocery store. Otherwise, common oregano will work fine.*

---

1. Fill a large pot with water and bring to a boil over high heat. Add the cauliflower and salt and boil for 12 to 14 minutes, until it's tender but still firm enough to stay intact. Transfer the cauliflower to a baking dish.

2. Preheat the oven to 450°F.

3. To make the marinade, heat the oil in a large sauté pan over medium heat. Add the onion and cook for 3 minutes on each side. Add the garlic cloves and cook for 1 to 2 minutes on each side, until golden. Add the peppercorns and cloves and cook, stirring continuously, for 1 minute. Add the guajillo chiles and cook for 20 seconds on each side. Add the broth, bay leaves, oregano, cumin, and allspice and simmer for 15 minutes.

4. Carefully transfer the contents of the pan to a blender. Add the chipotle peppers, pineapple chunks, vinegar, and salt and blend on high until smooth.

TO SERVE:

2 avocados, halved, pitted, peeled, and sliced

¼ small red onion, diced small

¼ bunch cilantro, chopped

2 limes, cut into wedges

Corn or flour tortillas, store-bought or homemade (pages 34 and 30), warmed

5. Using a basting brush, brush the cauliflower with the olive oil, then generously cover the cauliflower with the marinade, reserving about ¼ cup. Add the chopped pineapple to the reserved marinade, mix well, and add to the baking dish.

6. Roast for 24 minutes, checking on the cauliflower halfway through. If you notice any charring, cover with aluminum foil. Once done, the cauliflower should cut easily, like butter! If it doesn't, roast for another 5 to 6 minutes.

7. Garnish with the marinated baked pineapple pieces, sliced avocado, red onion, cilantro, and a squeeze of lime juice and serve with warm tortillas.

✲ CHILES RELLENOS DE PAPA Y QUESO ✲

Potato and Cheese-Stuffed Poblano Peppers

SERVES 6

STUFFED PEPPERS:

6 poblano peppers (sometimes labeled pasilla peppers)

1 pound Yukon Gold potatoes, peeled and diced

1 tablespoon plus ½ teaspoon sea salt, divided

1 (8-ounce) package shredded plant-based mozzarella cheese

2 tablespoons vegan butter

2 tablespoons plain, unsweetened plant-based milk

¼ cup Crema Mexicana (page 37) or store-bought vegan sour cream (optional)

2 cups Salsa Roja (page 75), divided

6 tablespoons neutral high-heat oil, such as avocado oil, divided

¼ bunch cilantro, chopped

BATTER:

1 cup all-purpose flour or gluten-free baking blend (such as Bob's Red Mill Gluten-Free 1-to-1 Baking Flour)

2 tablespoons cornstarch

1 teaspoon baking powder

1 teaspoon sea salt

1 teaspoon paprika

1 teaspoon garlic powder

1 cup sparkling water

I find all Mexican food incredibly comforting, but this dish in particular feels like a warm, cozy hug from my favorite person. Chiles rellenos are made with roasted poblano peppers, typically stuffed with either picadillo (ground meat) or cheese, then dipped in an egg batter and fried until golden and crisp before being smothered in a rich tomato sauce.

My Mexican American heritage really comes out to play with these chiles rellenos de papa y queso: one year, after Thanksgiving, mashed potato leftovers were sitting in the fridge and my husband and I were craving Mexican flavors. I stuffed some roasted poblano peppers with the mashed potatoes, added a bit of shredded vegan mozzarella cheese, dipped them in an egg-free batter, and made my Tía Chela's recipe for a classic, rich salsa roja. I am not the first to use potatoes as a filling for chiles rellenos, but I wish I was so I could take full credit for one of the most comforting dishes of all time.

---

1. Roast the poblano peppers on an open flame for 1 to 2 minutes, until charred on all sides. (Alternatively, heat the oven to the highest broiler setting, put the peppers on a rimmed baking sheet lined with aluminum foil, and broil on the middle oven rack for 1 to 2 minutes on each side, until charred.) Transfer the peppers to a bowl, cover with plastic wrap, and let sit for 10 minutes to release steam.

2. Meanwhile, put the potatoes in a medium pot, cover with water, and add 1 tablespoon salt. Bring to a boil over high heat and boil for 15 to 16 minutes, until the potatoes are fork-tender. Drain the potatoes and transfer to a large bowl. Add the cheese, butter, milk, crema or sour cream (if using), and remaining ½ teaspoon salt. Mash everything with a fork or potato masher until you reach a smooth consistency with some small chunks of potato still visible. Add ¼ cup salsa roja to the potatoes and mix again.

3. Remove the charred skin from the poblano peppers. Cut a slit down the side of each pepper and remove the seeds. Spoon a generous amount of the potato mixture inside each, then press the pepper closed.

4. In a medium bowl, whisk together all of the batter ingredients until there are no pockets of flour.

5. Heat the oil in a large, deep sauté pan over medium heat until it reaches 350°F. If you don't have a thermometer, you can drop about

½ teaspoon batter into the oil to test readiness. It should become a golden piece of fried dough in 50 to 60 seconds. If not ready, let the oil continue heating.

6. Dip a stuffed pepper into the batter, coating all sides. Add the coated pepper to the hot oil and fry for 3 minutes on each side, or until golden and crisp. Transfer the fried stuffed pepper to a paper towel–lined plate. Continue to batter and fry all the peppers, then wipe out the pan.

7. Pour the remaining 1¾ cups salsa roja into the same pan and gently simmer over low heat for 5 minutes. Add all the fried peppers to the pan. Serve each pepper with a generous amount of warm salsa spooned over the top and garnished with cilantro.

ENCHILADAS ROJAS DULCES

Sweet Red Enchiladas

SERVES 4

TOFU CHEESE:

1 (14- to 16-ounce) package firm tofu

4 tablespoons extra-virgin olive oil, divided

2 tablespoons fresh lemon juice

2 tablespoons nutritional yeast

½ teaspoon apple cider vinegar

½ teaspoon sea salt, divided

¼ medium white onion, roughly chopped

2 garlic cloves, roughly chopped

2 tablespoons hot water

SALSA:

5 guajillo chiles, stemmed and seeded

3 ancho chiles, stemmed and seeded

4 cups water

½ (3.3-ounce) disk Mexican chocolate (such as Ibarra), roughly chopped

4 whole black peppercorns

1-inch piece cinnamon stick, broken into pieces

1 large garlic clove, peeled

1 (1-inch) piece piloncillo *or* 2 tablespoons brown sugar

1 oregano sprig

½ teaspoon sea salt

2 tablespoons neutral, such as avocado oil

If you've had enchiladas in the US, you've probably had them Tex-Mex style, which consists of flour tortillas doused in a store-bought red enchilada sauce, covered in cheddar cheese, and baked in a casserole dish. But authentic Mexican enchiladas showcase our indigenous roots, always starting with the corn tortilla as the foundation and using a chile-based salsa. The tortillas are stuffed with anything from animal protein to potatoes to cheese, and are *sometimes* baked, although the tortillas are more often fried before or after being submerged in salsa, then rolled around the filling and served right away.

My Tía Pilla's enchiladas rojas dulces are special in that this chile-based salsa has a unique touch of Mexican chocolate and whole spices, making for the most divine, complex, spicy, and slightly sweet experience. My tía would typically stuff these with queso enchilado (a Mexican goat's milk cheese) and finely diced onion. For a plant-based alternative, I stuff them with homemade tofu cheese, although you can also use your favorite soft vegan cheese; I particularly love the fresh mozzarella by Miyoko's. My tofu cheese resembles the Mexican version of ricotta cheese—requesón—and works as a stand-alone plant-based cheese in other recipes as well.

---

1. To make the tofu cheese, wrap the tofu in a kitchen towel or paper towel and gently squeeze for 10 to 15 seconds to remove the excess water. Crumble the tofu into a large bowl. Add 2 tablespoons olive oil, the lemon juice, nutritional yeast, vinegar, and ¼ teaspoon salt. Mix well and set aside.

2. Heat the remaining 2 tablespoons oil in a medium skillet over medium heat. Add the onion and sauté for 5 minutes, or until golden and slightly charred. Add the garlic and sauté for 2 to 3 minutes, until golden. Transfer the onion, garlic, and any oil left in the pan to a blender, along with the hot water and remaining ¼ teaspoon salt. Blend on high until smooth, then pour over the tofu. Mix well and set aside. Wipe out the pan and blender.

3. To make the salsa, put the chiles and water in a medium pot. Bring to a boil over high heat, then boil for 10 minutes. Drain, reserving about 2 cups of the cooking liquid.

(Continued)

(Continued)

ENCHILADAS:

¼ cup neutral high-heat oil, such as avocado oil

10 corn tortillas, store-bought or homemade (page 34)

TO SERVE:

Crema Mexicana (page 37) or store-bought vegan sour cream

Queso Cotija (page 38) or store-bought vegan feta

2 avocados, halved, pitted, peeled, and sliced

¼ bunch cilantro, chopped

¼ small white onion, thinly sliced

4. Transfer the softened chiles and 1½ cups of the reserved cooking liquid to the blender, along with the Mexican chocolate, peppercorns, cinnamon pieces, garlic, piloncillo, oregano, and salt. Blend on high for 1 minute, or until smooth.

5. Heat the oil in a medium sauté pan over medium-low heat. Hold a fine-mesh strainer over the pan and pour the contents of the blender through it, then discard the solids in the strainer. Bring the salsa to a simmer, then turn the heat down to low. If the salsa seems too thick, add ¼ cup more cooking liquid to loosen it to the consistency of marinara sauce.

6. To assemble the enchiladas, heat the oil in the skillet over medium-high heat. Add a tortilla and fry for 20 to 30 seconds on each side, until golden and slightly crispy but still pliable. Remove the tortilla from the oil with tongs and let the excess oil drip off, then drench the tortilla in the salsa. Transfer the salsa-dipped tortilla to a serving dish. Add 2 spoonfuls of the tofu cheese filling down one side of the tortilla, roll like a taquito, then spoon more salsa over the top. Repeat to fry, fill, and roll the remaining tortillas. To serve, drizzle with crema, sprinkle with Cotija cheese, and top with sliced avocado, chopped cilantro, and sliced onion.

✻ ENCHILADAS SUIZAS ✻

Creamy Green Enchiladas

MAKES 10 ENCHILADAS

2 (20-ounce) cans green jackfruit in brine, drained and rinsed

1 small yellow onion, thinly sliced

4 garlic cloves, peeled, 2 left whole and 2 minced

4 tablespoons neutral oil, such as avocado oil, divided

Sea salt and ground black pepper

3½ cups Salsa Verde (page 81), divided

½ cup Crema Mexicana (page 37) or store-bought vegan sour cream, plus more for serving

10 corn tortillas, store-bought or homemade (page 34)

1 (8-ounce) package shredded vegan mozzarella cheese

¼ bunch cilantro, chopped

Every Mexican family has a dish they excel in, and this is my family's. Enchiladas suizas make it onto the menu a handful of times a month, especially for family dinners with relatives. It's a magical combination of tortillas submerged in a creamy tomatillo salsa, traditionally stuffed with shredded chicken, then rolled, topped with cheese and crema Mexicana, and baked in the oven.

Despite the name, the dish does not have Swiss roots—in fact, its origins are said to be with a chef in Mexico City in the 1950s. While enchiladas verdes (made with green salsa) were already around for centuries by this point, this chef added melty cheese and crema... but no one is quite sure how that led to "Swiss" being included in the name! What we do know, however, is that this is a recipe that will live on in my family for decades to come. It was the very first family recipe I "veganized" nearly 10 years ago because I knew I could not lose this delicious part of my culture when I gave up animal products.

I tested many filling, cheese, and crema replacements to make this as authentic as possible. In place of chicken I use jackfruit, a meaty plant-based alternative to shredded animal protein. My cashew "crema" is an equally delicious alternative—I dare a single dairy lover to disagree—and these days there are many great vegan cheeses available in supermarkets. So with just a handful of plant-based adjustments, I can hold on tight to this dish forever.

---

1. Put the jackfruit in a large bowl and remove the soft seed inside each piece, then discard. Transfer the jackfruit to a large pot. Cover with water (about 5 inches above the jackfruit) and add one-quarter of the sliced onion and the whole garlic cloves. Bring to a boil over medium heat and cook for 20 minutes. Drain in a colander and rinse under cool running water. Put the jackfruit, onion, and garlic in the center of a thin kitchen towel or in a nut milk bag and form into a bundle. Squeeze to press out all the liquid. Transfer the jackfruit, onion, and garlic to a cutting board and roughly chop.

2. Heat 1 tablespoon oil in a large sauté pan over medium-low heat. Add the rest of the sliced onion and sauté for 4 minutes, then add the minced garlic and sauté for 1 minute. Transfer the onion and garlic to a bowl.

(Continued)

(Continued)

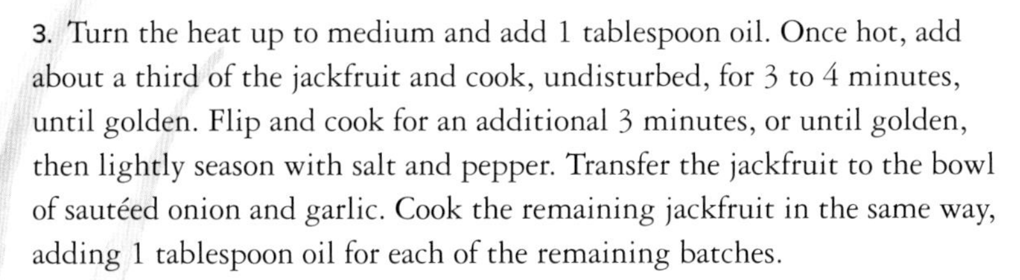

3. Turn the heat up to medium and add 1 tablespoon oil. Once hot, add about a third of the jackfruit and cook, undisturbed, for 3 to 4 minutes, until golden. Flip and cook for an additional 3 minutes, or until golden, then lightly season with salt and pepper. Transfer the jackfruit to the bowl of sautéed onion and garlic. Cook the remaining jackfruit in the same way, adding 1 tablespoon oil for each of the remaining batches.

4. Once the last batch is cooked, return all the jackfruit to the pan, along with the onion and garlic. Pour in ½ cup salsa verde, mix to combine, and cook for 5 minutes, or until the salsa thickens. Remove the pan from the heat.

5. Preheat the oven to 375°F.

6. Combine the remaining 3 cups salsa verde and the crema in a blender and blend on high for 1 minute, or until smooth and creamy.

7. Coat the bottom of a casserole dish with about ¼ cup of the blended creamy salsa verde and spread evenly. Set aside.

8. Heat a large skillet or comal over high heat. Add a tortilla and cook for 30 to 40 seconds on each side, then transfer to a work surface. Add 2 spoonfuls of the jackfruit mixture down the middle of the tortilla and roll tight, then place in the casserole dish seam side down. Repeat with the remaining tortillas and filling. Pour 2 cups creamy salsa verde on top. Top with the shredded cheese, cover with aluminum foil, and bake for 30 minutes, or until the cheese is melted. Serve with a generous drizzle of crema, top with cilantro, and add more creamy salsa verde to your liking.

POZOLE VERDE

SERVES 8

50 ounces canned hominy, drained and rinsed

10 cups low-sodium vegetable broth

1 head garlic, top ¼ inch sliced off to expose cloves

2 bay leaves

2 poblano peppers (sometimes labeled pasilla peppers)

4 tablespoons neutral oil, such as avocado oil, divided

12 tomatillos, husked

¾ medium white onion, cut into 3 pieces

2 serrano peppers, stemmed

½ cup baby spinach

¼ bunch cilantro

¼ cup pumpkin seeds

1 tablespoon dried Mexican oregano or regular oregano

½ teaspoon dried epazote

1 cup water

4 tablespoons vegan butter, divided

4 portobello mushroom caps, cut into ¼-inch-thick slices

Sea salt

TO SERVE:

½ green cabbage, finely shredded

¼ medium white onion, finely diced

2 avocados, halved, pitted, peeled, and sliced

I have fond memories of walking into either of my grandmothers' kitchens and smelling that distinctly aromatic, transportive scent in the air as I laid my eyes on the large steel pots of pozole bubbling on the stovetop. A traditional, hearty Mexican stew, pozole is based around the star indigenous ingredient of hominy, or whole kernels of dried corn (known as maize), that have been nixtamalized in the same process used to make tortillas. Hominy is plump, starchy, and buttery, and has a very different texture and provides a different experience from that of fresh sweet corn. Pozole traditionally comes in three different types of broth—red, green, or white—the three options together representing the Mexican flag. In my Grandma Esther's home we would be served a bowl of pozole blanco (white) de pollo (chicken), while in my Abuelita Eva's home, we would be served a pozole rojo (red) de puerco (pork).

As with many traditional Mexican dishes, the foundation of a pozole lies with the plants: hominy, chiles, and spices, and vegetable-forward toppings take this dish to the next level. But a central ingredient that plays a big role in flavor and the distinct richness is whichever animal protein is used, so I had my work cut out for me in creating a vegan pozole that would reflect the layers of flavor, richness, and warmth my grandmothers' had.

The answer was pozole verde, a green broth packed with a variety of herbs, aromatics, and pumpkin seeds, making for an explosion of mouthwatering flavor. Thickly sliced portobello mushrooms add a wonderful umami, meaty element, making this pozole verde a nutritious and also irresistibly delicious bowl of comfort to feed to anyone you love. *Note: Hominy comes in many different can sizes, so to get about 50 ounces, you might need three 15.5-ounce cans, two 29-ounce cans, or half of a 108-ounce can.*

---

1. Combine the hominy, broth, garlic head, and bay leaves in a large pot and bring to a boil over high heat. Boil for 30 minutes.

2. Meanwhile, roast the poblano peppers on an open flame for 1 to 2 minutes, until charred on all sides. (Alternatively, heat the oven to the highest broiler setting, put the peppers on a rimmed baking sheet lined

(Continued)

(Continued)

2 radishes, thinly sliced

4 limes, cut into wedges

8 tostadas *or* 1 (10- to 12-ounce) bag tortilla chips

with aluminum foil, and broil on the middle rack for 1 to 2 minutes on each side, until charred.) Transfer the peppers to a bowl, cover with plastic wrap, and let sit for 10 minutes to release steam.

3. While the hominy boils and the poblanos steam, heat 2 tablespoons oil in a large cast-iron skillet over medium heat. Add the tomatillos, onion, and serrano peppers and cook, undisturbed, for 4 to 5 minutes, allowing the ingredients to char, then flip and cook for an additional 4 to 5 minutes to char the other side as well. Transfer all the roasted ingredients to a blender. Wipe out the pan.

4. Remove the charred skin, stems, inner ribs, and seeds from the poblano peppers. Add the peppers to the blender, along with the spinach, cilantro, pumpkin seeds, oregano, epazote, and water and blend on high until smooth.

5. Once the hominy has boiled for 30 minutes, pour the blended mixture into the pot, turn the heat down to medium, and simmer for 20 minutes.

6. Meanwhile, heat 1 tablespoon oil and 1 tablespoon butter in the cast-iron skillet over medium heat. Add one-quarter of the mushrooms and cook, undisturbed, for 3 to 4 minutes, until golden, then flip and cook for an additional 3 to 4 minutes, lightly seasoning with salt. Transfer the mushrooms to the simmering hominy. Cook the remaining mushrooms in the same way, adding more oil and butter to the skillet for each batch and transferring the mushrooms to the hominy as they are done. Taste and add more salt to taste.

7. Spoon the pozole into bowls, top with cabbage, onion, avocado, radish, and a squeeze of lime, and serve with a side of tostadas or tortilla chips.

CHILES EN NOGADA

Sweet and Savory Stuffed Poblano Peppers

SERVES 8

SAUCE:

¾ cup raw or roasted walnuts

½ cup raw or roasted cashews

1¼ cup plain, unsweetened plant-based milk

½ teaspoon cane sugar

½ teaspoon sea salt

STUFFED PEPPERS:

8 poblano peppers (sometimes labeled pasilla peppers)

5 tablespoons neutral high-heat oil, such as avocado divided

1 pound cremini mushrooms, finely diced

Sea salt

1 green plantain, peeled and finely diced

1 medium white onion, finely diced

3 garlic cloves, minced

2 ripe Roma tomatoes, finely diced

1 red apple, cored and finely diced

1 pear, cored and finely diced

1 cup cooked green lentils

¾ cup low-sodium vegetable broth

¼ cup raisins

1 teaspoon dried oregano

¼ teaspoon ground cumin

Although Cinco de Mayo has become the most prominent day to celebrate Mexican culture in the States, it is not actually the Mexican independence day it is sometimes misunderstood to be. May 5 marks the anniversary of the 1862 victory of Mexican troops over French forces in Puebla, but it is actually barely celebrated south of the border. The true Mexican Independence Day is September 16, commemorating the day in 1810 when Catholic priest Don Miguel Hidalgo y Costilla rang the bells to call the Mexican people to take up arms again the Spanish, and the entire country comes out to celebrate.

In the month of September, I always find myself in Mexico just in time to celebrate this day. There is an extra special energy in the air as people prepare for days of festivities, lots of food, fireworks, and el grito, a gathering that occurs on the eve of Independence Day. This celebration occurs mainly in Mexico City's famous public square, Zócalo, with locals gathering to proudly chant "Viva Mexico, viva la independencia!" Every restaurant in Mexico advertises their version of chiles en nogada, a dish that commemorates the holiday.

It has been said that when Mexico gained independence from Spain in the early 1800s, nuns in Puebla created this unique dish for the leader of the Mexican Army: roasted poblano peppers stuffed with a savory and sweet picadillo of meat, fruits, and nuts, smothered in a creamy, nutty sauce, and topped with pomegranate seeds—the pomegranate, sauce, and pepper making up the red, white, and green of Mexico's flag. While a plant-based ground meat would be a great substitute for the animal protein typically used in the picadillo, I chose to keep the foundation of the dish rooted in plants and deployed minced mushrooms for an earthy, umami filling that plays beautifully with the sweetness of the fresh and dried fruits. Beyond being delicious, this dish represents Mexican patriotism and pride in the beauty, flavors, and colors of our country.

---

1. To start the sauce, put the walnuts and cashews in a medium bowl. Cover with boiling water and set aside to soak while you prepare the peppers.

(Continued)

(Continued)

TO SERVE:

½ cup pomegranate seeds

¼ bunch cilantro, chopped

2. Roast the poblano peppers on an open flame for 1 to 2 minutes, until charred on all sides. (Alternatively, heat the oven to the highest broiler setting, put the peppers on a rimmed baking sheet lined with aluminum foil, and broil on the middle rack for 1 to 2 minutes on each side, until charred.) Transfer the peppers to a bowl, cover with plastic wrap, and let sit for 10 minutes to release steam.

3. Meanwhile, heat 1 tablespoon oil in a large skillet or sauté pan over medium heat. Add one-third of the mushrooms and cook, undisturbed, for 3 minutes, or until golden. Flip the mushrooms, lightly sprinkle with salt, and cook for an additional 3 minutes. Transfer the mushrooms to a bowl. Cook the remaining mushrooms in the same way, adding another 1 tablespoon oil to the pan for each batch and transferring the mushrooms to the bowl as they are done.

4. Heat the remaining 2 tablespoons oil in the same pan over medium heat. Add the plantain and cook for 2 minutes on each side, or until golden. Transfer to the bowl with the mushrooms. Add the onion to the pan and sauté for 3 minutes. Add the garlic and sauté for 1 minute. Add the tomatoes and sauté for 5 minutes. Add the apple and pear and sauté everything together for 7 minutes. Add the cooked lentils, broth, and raisins and simmer for 10 minutes, or until the liquid is mostly absorbed. Return the mushrooms and plantain to the pan, along with the oregano and cumin, and season with salt to taste. Turn the heat down to low.

5. Remove the charred skin from the poblano peppers. Cut a slit down the side of each pepper and remove the seeds. Spoon a generous amount of the mushroom filling inside each, then press the peppers closed.

6. To finish the sauce, drain the cashews and walnuts and rinse under cool running water. Combine the nuts, milk, sugar, and salt in a blender and blend on high for 1 minute, or until smooth.

7. To serve, place a stuffed pepper on each plate, cover with the creamy sauce, and top with pomegranate seeds and chopped cilantro.

ENMOLADAS DE PLATANO MACHO

Plantain Enmoladas

SERVES 4

FILLING:

4 ripe (yellow to nearly black) plantains, peeled and cut into 4 or 5 chunks

1 teaspoon sea salt, divided

2 tablespoons vegan butter

¼ cup Crema Mexicana (page 37) or store-bought vegan sour cream

ENMOLADAS:

Mole Negro (page 159—without the roasted mushrooms) or Mole Rojo (page 165—without the roasted cauliflower) *or* 1 (16-ounce) jar black mole paste mixed with 3 cups low-sodium vegetable broth

4 tablespoons neutral high-heat oil, such as avocado oil, divided

16 corn tortillas, store-bought or homemade (page 34)

¾ cup Crema Mexicana (page 37) or store-bought vegan sour cream

2 tablespoons sesame seeds

If I had to choose my last meal on Earth, it would be this one. When I am traveling in Oaxaca, I find myself wanting to eat the same thing for breakfast, lunch, and dinner; while the vegan scene in Oaxaca is not as abundant as it is in other parts of Mexico, one dish that I can always count on is enmoladas de platano macho. This dish is similar to enchiladas, except that enchiladas are smothered with a chile-based salsa, and enmoladas are smothered in mole—it's right in the names! Oaxaca is one of the birthplaces of mole, and they are known for their seven varieties: negro, rojo, amarillo, verde, coloradito, estofado, and chichilo. Every family and restaurant has its own unique recipe, which is a great source of pride.

This variety is part of the reason that I could never get tired of this dish, but I would choose it as my last meal because I didn't grow up eating it at home, so it feels like a special treat I only have when traveling. Enmoladas are usually stuffed with chicken, but plantains are a common alternative for a delicious plant-based substitute—the spicy-sweet-savory complexity of the mole complements the creamy heartiness of plantains. While any mole can be used for this recipe, I recommend mole negro or mole rojo.

---

1. Put the plantains in a medium pot, cover with water, and add ¾ teaspoon salt. Bring to a boil over high heat. Boil for 10 minutes, or until fork-tender; the plantains should be the texture of a ripe banana. Drain and transfer the plantains to a medium bowl. Add the butter, crema, and remaining ¼ teaspoon salt. Using a large fork or potato masher, mash and combine all the ingredients until mostly smooth with some small bits of plantain visible. Taste and add more salt if needed.

2. Put the homemade mole (or jarred mole paste and broth) in the same pot and bring to a simmer over medium-low heat. Turn the heat down to low.

3. Heat 2 tablespoons oil in a large sauté pan over medium heat. Add a tortilla and fry for 12 to 15 seconds on each side, then dip into the mole. Transfer the coated tortilla to a plate, add a generous spoonful of the plantain mixture to one side of the tortilla, and roll it up into a taquito. Transfer to a platter seam side down. Repeat to make the remaining enmoladas, adding more oil to the pan as needed.

4. Serve 3 or 4 enmoladas per person, covered with more warm mole, drizzled with crema, and garnished with a sprinkle of sesame seeds.

POSTRES

Desserts

✻ CAJETA ✻

Mexican Caramel

MAKES 1 CUP

Cajeta is a traditional Mexican caramel made from goat's milk flavored with cinnamon and vanilla. This sticky, thick, sweet deliciousness is from the state of Guanajuato. Full-fat oat milk in place of the goat's milk is key for this vegan version! An even layer of cajeta spread on toast is such a tasty treat, and it makes for a perfect dipping sauce alongside homemade Churros (page 217).

---

4 cups plus 1 tablespoon full-fat oat milk, divided

¾ cup brown sugar

⅛ teaspoon sea salt

1 teaspoon vanilla extract

1 cinnamon stick

½ teaspoon baking soda

1. In a medium pot, combine 4 cups oat milk, the brown sugar, salt, vanilla, and cinnamon stick. Bring to a simmer over medium heat and cook for about 10 minutes.

2. Meanwhile, in a small cup or bowl, whisk together the baking soda and remaining 1 tablespoon oat milk.

3. Remove the pot from the heat (but don't turn the heat off) and whisk in the baking soda and milk mixture. Once the bubbling (from the baking soda) subsides, return the pot to the heat. Lay a wooden spoon or spatula across the pot to help prevent it from boiling over. Cook for 45 minutes, stirring every few minutes, then remove the cinnamon stick.

4. Turn the heat down to low and continue cooking, stirring every few minutes, for 50 more minutes, or until a thick caramelly consistency is reached. Keep in mind, the cajeta will thicken much more after sitting in the fridge. Use right away or store in a covered container in the fridge for up to 1 week.

LECHERA

Sweetened Condensed Milk

MAKES 1 CUP

Lechera—sweetened condensed milk—is a deliciously creamy, sweet condiment used in a lot of Mexican desserts like Chocoflan (page 204) and Rollos de Fresas con Crema (page 208), but it can also be stirred into a cup of coffee for a sweet pick-me-up or drizzled over fresh fruit for a simple and quick dessert. The process takes patience, but I promise it is worth it! Put on a relaxing album (I really enjoy Silvana Estrada, a Mexican musician providing calming indie tunes) and take a moment to be present in the kitchen as you slowly create magical sweetness.

---

1 (13.5-ounce) can full-fat coconut milk or coconut cream

½ cup cane sugar

1 tablespoon brown sugar

⅛ teaspoon sea salt

2 tablespoons plain, unsweetened plant-based milk

½ teaspoon vanilla extract

1. Combine the coconut milk, sugars, and salt in a medium pot. Heat over medium-low heat for 45 minutes, stirring every 5 minutes. The mixture should reach a thickened yet still runny consistency.

2. Remove the pot from the heat and let sit for 5 minutes. Add the milk and vanilla and whisk vigorously. Use right away or store in a covered container in the fridge for up to 2 weeks. The mixture will thicken and turn whiter after refrigeration, like traditional lechera.

※ CHOCOFLAN ※

Caramel Custard Chocolate Cake

SERVES 12

1 cup cane sugar

1 (16-ounce) package silken tofu, drained

1 cup Lechera (page 203) or canned vegan condensed milk

¼ cup plain, unsweetened plant-based milk

2 teaspoons vanilla extract

½ teaspoon sea salt

⅓ cup cornstarch

1½ teaspoons agar agar powder

⅛ teaspoon ground turmeric

1 (13.25-ounce) box chocolate cake mix (such as Betty Crocker), plus plant-based ingredients as needed (see headnote)

1½ tablespoons apple cider vinegar

This caramel custard dessert layered with dreamy rich chocolate cake is one of the most beloved treats in Mexican homes. My mission to create a vegan version of this special cake meant I couldn't stop until it was as good as my mom's. Traditionally, flan is created with a lot of eggs and copious amounts of dairy. I wanted to achieve the same silky, creamy texture my mom's flan has, and found that replacing the eggs with silken tofu, cornstarch, and a key ingredient, agar agar powder (a plant-based alternative to gelatin that can be purchased online), was the answer. I also took my mom's advice and leaned on a boxed cake mix for the chocolate cake layer, to save time. When following the instructions on the cake mix box, simply swap the eggs for applesauce (1 egg = ¼ cup applesauce) and replace any milk or butter with plant-based versions (many boxed mixes call for water, but I always replace that with plant-based milk). Overall, this cake is impressive in presentation and flavor, and while it does take patience and time, it requires very minimal active effort and is a no-brainer for sharing with your favorite people. *Note: You will need a 10- to 12-cup Bundt pan to make this cake—it will not work in any other pan. No need to grease.*

---

1. Preheat the oven to 350°F.

2. Put the sugar in a large sauté pan and heat over medium heat, stirring continuously, for 5 to 6 minutes, until the sugar melts and forms a caramel: you're looking for a light golden color. Be careful to not let it get too dark, which will taste bitter. Immediately pour the caramel into a 10- to 12-cup Bundt pan and, using oven mitts, pick up the pan and swirl it around to evenly coat the bottom with the caramel. Set aside.

3. Combine the silken tofu, lechera, milk, vanilla, and salt in a blender and blend on high for 1 minute, or until smooth. Hold a fine-mesh sifter over the blender and sift the cornstarch, agar agar powder, and turmeric into the blender. Blend on high for 1 minute. Using a spatula, scrape the walls of the blender to ensure all the cornstarch gets blended in. Blend again for 10 seconds, then pour the contents of the blender into the Bundt pan.

(Continued)

(Continued)

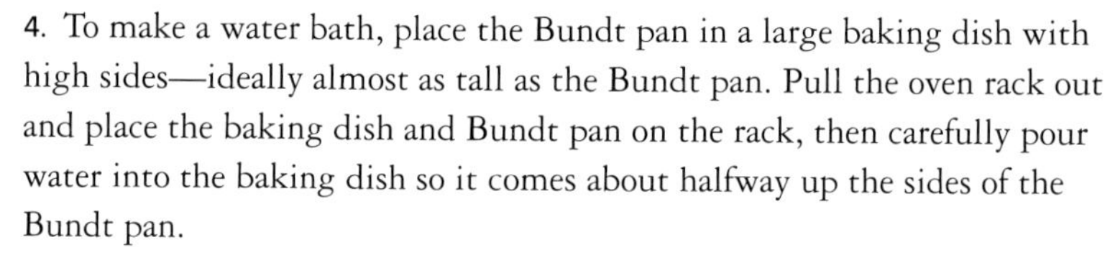

4. To make a water bath, place the Bundt pan in a large baking dish with high sides—ideally almost as tall as the Bundt pan. Pull the oven rack out and place the baking dish and Bundt pan on the rack, then carefully pour water into the baking dish so it comes about halfway up the sides of the Bundt pan.

5. Bake for 1 hour. Remove the Bundt pan from the oven, leaving the water bath in the oven and the oven on.

6. Follow the instructions on the cake mix box to make the batter, substituting plant-based ingredients as necessary and adding the vinegar. Slowly pour the batter over the baked flan.

7. Carefully place the Bundt pan back into the water bath in the oven and bake for 50 minutes. Check for doneness by sticking a toothpick in the middle—it should come out clean. If not, bake for another 10 to 15 minutes.

8. Let the chocoflan cool for 2 hours, then cover with aluminum foil and refrigerate for at least 6 hours.

9. When ready to serve, run a kitchen towel under hot water and squeeze mostly dry. Lay the hot dampened towel on the counter and place the Bundt pan on top, lifting the towel up to surround the base of the Bundt pan and warm the surface. This will help melt the caramel layer. Keep the towel there for a minute.

10. Remove the foil and carefully run a butter knife around the edges of the chocoflan. Place a large serving dish upside down over the pan, then carefully flip the pan onto the plate. Set the plate on the counter and carefully lift the pan to release the chocoflan. You may have to wiggle it a tiny bit to release.

CALABAZA EN TACHA

SERVES 4

Calabaza en tacha is the most blissful experience: it melts in your mouth like a custard or pumpkin pie, and it could not be simpler to make. A pre-Hispanic dessert using the "en tacha" method (cooked in syrup), it was traditionally prepared by the Indigenous people around Día de Muertos (Day of the Dead, called Mikailwitl and Wey Mikailwitl in Indigenous Mesoamerican tradition) as an offering to their ancestors who had passed on. The Indigenous people were said to have cooked the squash in honey over a firepit oven, although these days piloncillo is often used instead of honey, making this dessert naturally vegan.

---

1 butternut or kabocha squash, peeled, seeded, and cut into chunks

2 cups water

1 (8-ounce) piece piloncillo *or* 1 cup brown sugar

4 whole cloves

1 cinnamon stick

1 tablespoon vanilla extract

½ teaspoon sea salt

Plain, unsweetened plant-based milk, for serving

Flaky sea salt, for serving (optiona

1. Combine the squash, water, piloncillo, cloves, cinnamon stick, vanilla, and salt in a large pot. Cover and cook over medium heat for 15 minutes.
2. Move the lid an inch to the side to release steam and continue to cook, stirring every 5 minutes, for 30 minutes, or until the squash is caramelized and soft. The water should have mostly reduced to a syrup by this point.
3. Serve the candied squash in bowls with a splash of milk and an optional sprinkle of flaky sea salt on top.

ROLLOS DE FRESAS CON CREMA

Strawberries and Cream Cinnamon Rolls

MAKES 12 ROLLS

DOUGH:

2 cups plain, unsweetened plant-based milk, divided

¼ cup plus 1 tablespoon cane sugar, divided

1 (¼-ounce) packet active dry yeast (2¼ teaspoons)

5 cups all-purpose flour, divided, plus more for dusting

1 cup melted vegan butter, plus 1 tablespoon softened vegan butter

2 teaspoons vanilla exact

1 teaspoon baking powder

1 teaspoon sea salt

1 teaspoon neutral oil, such as avocado oil, or additional vegan butter

FILLING:

½ cup vegan butter, softened

1 cup brown sugar

2 teaspoons ground cinnamon

TOPPING:

1 cup Lechera (page 203) or canned vegan condensed milk

1 pound strawberries, hulled and diced

Fresas con crema is a classic, simple, and beloved Mexican dessert consisting of fresh strawberries served with a sweet cream. I thought how delicious that combo would be on top of warm, gooey, fluffy cinnamon rolls, and this recipe was born. Many rollos de canela (cinnamon rolls) were consumed from a small café in Mexico City during my time living there in my early 20s, and these take me right back to those memories. Instead of icing, the rolls are drizzled with lechera (sweetened condensed milk) and fresh strawberries. I especially love to make these for holiday brunches, either to munch on while the rest of the food cooks or as a sweet something to end with.

---

1. In a small heatproof bowl, microwave 1 cup milk for 1 minute, until warm to the touch but not hot. (Alternatively, heat the milk in a small saucepan over low heat.)

2. Transfer the warm milk to a large bowl, add 1 tablespoon cane sugar and the yeast, and mix well. Set aside for 10 minutes; the yeast should be foaming. Add the remaining ¼ cup cane sugar, 2 cups flour, and another ½ cup milk and whisk until smooth. Add the remaining ½ cup milk, melted butter, vanilla, baking powder, and salt and mix well. Add the remaining 3 cups flour about ½ cup at a time, mixing continuously with your hands until fully incorporated. Form the dough into a slightly sticky ball.

3. Dust a work surface generously with flour. Place the dough ball on the floured surface and knead for 7 minutes. The dough should be soft and no longer sticky; add up to ¼ cup more flour if needed.

4. Wash and dry the same bowl, then grease it with the oil. Place the dough in the greased bowl and cover with a kitchen towel or plastic wrap. Let sit in a warm, dark place for 1 hour; the dough should roughly double in size.

5. Remove the towel and punch down the dough. Lightly flour a large work surface and a rolling pin. Roll out the dough into a rectangle about 12 by 8 inches.

6. For the filling, spread the softened butter over the dough, being sure to go right to the edges. In a small bowl, combine the brown sugar and cinnamon. Evenly spread the mixture with your hands in an even layer over the buttered dough.

7. Starting with a long side, roll up the dough into a 12-inch log. Cut the log into 1-inch segments using unflavored dental floss or a sharp knife.

8. Grease a 9 x 13-inch baking dish (or two 5 x 7-inch loaf pans) with 1 tablespoon softened butter. Place the rolls cut side down in the greased baking dish(es). Cover with a kitchen towel and let rise for 30 minutes. Meanwhile, preheat the oven to 350°F.

9. Remove the towel and bake for 18 to 22 minutes, until the tops are barely golden brown. While the rolls are still hot, generously drizzle with lechera and top with fresh strawberries.

CONCHAS

Sweet Bread Rolls

MAKES 12 PASTRIES

DOUGH:

2 cups plain, unsweetened plant-based milk, divided

½ cup plus 1 tablespoon cane sugar

1 (¼-ounce) packet active dry yeast (2¼ teaspoons)

5 cups all purpose-flour, divided, plus more for dusting

1 cup melted vegan butter

1 tablespoon baking powder

2 teaspoons vanilla extract

1 teaspoon sea salt

1 teaspoon neutral oil, such as avocado oil, or additional vegan butter

SUGAR TOPPING:

¼ cup dried hibiscus flowers

½ cup water

⅔ cup vegetable shortening

½ teaspoon vanilla extract

⅔ cup plus 2 tablespoons all-purpose flour

⅔ cup cane sugar

I have the warmest memory in my mind of my Grandma Esther on our front doorstep with a smile on her face and a pink box in her hands, filled with pan dulce (sweet bread), a treat for after dinner and likely a part of breakfast the next morning as well. Conchas are a classic pan dulce that are round, fluffy, soft, and buttery and have a subtle sweetness from the sugar topping laid out in the shell-like shape that gives these rolls their name. The city I grew up in is filled with panaderías (bakeries), so pan dulce was rarely missing from our family's homes, especially around the holiday season. The sugar topping on the classic concha is either dark chocolate for the cocoa flavor, white for vanilla, or a bright pink strawberry color—sometimes just a dye but sometimes a real fruit flavor. I wanted to utilize a natural plant ingredient that would be an alternative to a food coloring dye, so I opted for flor de jamaica (dried hibiscus flower) to create a beautiful blush rose color. These pastries *must* be served with a hot cup of Café de Olla (page 231), Champurrado (page 234), or hot chocolate.

---

1. In a small heatproof bowl, microwave 1 cup milk for 1 minute, until warm to the touch but not hot. (Alternatively, heat the milk in a small saucepan over low heat.)

2. Transfer the warm milk to a small bowl, add 1 tablespoon cane sugar and the yeast, and mix well. Set aside for 10 minutes; the yeast should be foaming.

3. In a large bowl, whisk together the remaining 1 cup milk, remaining ½ cup sugar, 2 cups flour, and the melted butter. Set aside for 10 minutes.

4. Add the yeast mixture to the flour mixture and whisk until smooth. Add the baking powder, vanilla, and salt and mix again. Add the remaining 3 cups flour about ½ cup at a time, mixing continuously with your hands until fully incorporated. Form the dough into a slightly sticky ball.

5. Dust a work surface generously with flour. Place the dough on the floured surface and knead for 7 minutes. The dough should be soft and no longer sticky; add up to ¼ cup more flour if needed.

(Continued)

(Continued)

6. Wash and dry the same bowl, then grease it with the oil. Place the dough in the greased bowl and cover with a kitchen towel or plastic wrap. Let sit in a warm, dark place for 1½ hours; the dough should roughly double in size.

7. While the dough is rising, make the sugar topping. In a small pot, combine the hibiscus flowers and water and bring to a boil over medium-high heat. Boil for 5 minutes, then turn the heat down to medium-low and simmer for 20 minutes. Remove the pot from the heat and set aside to cool for 30 minutes. This is your jamaica concentrate.

8. Transfer 1 teaspoon jamaica concentrate to a medium bowl, add the vegetable shortening and vanilla, and mix well to combine. Add the flour and sugar and mix until a soft dough forms. (This will result in a pale pink color; if you want a deeper pink, add another 1 teaspoon jamaica concentrate and another 1 tablespoon flour. The remaining jamaica concentrate can be stored in a covered container in the refrigerator for up to 4 days.) Divide the sugar topping into 12 balls. Cover with plastic wrap.

9. Line two baking pans with parchment paper. Once the dough has risen, divide the dough into 12 even pieces and roll each piece into a smooth ball between your hands. Place the dough balls in the prepared baking pans, leaving 2 inches space between each roll. Gently press down on each roll to flatten slightly.

10. Flatten a ball of sugar topping into a circle the same size as the pastry and place it on a pastry roll. Using the tip of a butter knife, cut a seashell design. Repeat with the remaining sugar topping. Cover the conchas with plastic wrap and let rise for 35 minutes. Meanwhile, preheat the oven to 350°F.

11. Bake the conchas for 22 minutes, or until lightly golden on the sides. Let cool for 30 minutes before serving. Store leftovers in a covered container for up to 5 days.

PASTEL TRES LECHES

Tres Leches Cake

SERVES 8

CAKE:

1 tablespoon vegan butter, softened, or neutral oil, such as avocado oil, for greasing

Homemade

2 cups cane sugar

2 cups plain, unsweetened plant-based milk

½ cup + 2 tablespoons melted vegan butter or neutral oil, such as avocado oil

½ cup unsweetened applesauce

1½ tablespoons white vinegar or apple cider vinegar

1 tablespoon vanilla extract

3½ cups all-purpose flour

2 teaspoons baking soda

¾ teaspoon sea salt

Cake mix

1 (13.25-ounce) box vanilla or yellow cake mix (such as Betty Crocker), plus plant-based ingredients as needed (see headnote)

1½ tablespoons apple cider vinegar

The most delicate, next-level-moist, custard-like experience you can possibly find in a cake, this fluffy vanilla confection is bathed in a creamy mixture of three different types of milk—traditionally a combination of whole, evaporated, and condensed milks. To make this sweet memory come to life in my vegan kitchen, I had to first and foremost make a call to my loving Tía Lucia, the baking queen in our family. I used her recipe as a guide and made some simple dairy and egg swaps. For our three milks, I used homemade lechera (although a store-bought canned vegan condensed milk can be used as well) and a combination of oat and soy milks, for their respective creaminess and natural sweetness (although any two plant-based milks will do). Starting with a homemade cake makes for a divine tres leches, but for an easy hack, you can opt for a store-bought cake mix, as most are in fact vegan! I've included instructions for both below. When following the instructions on the box, simply swap the eggs for applesauce (1 egg = ¼ cup applesauce) and replace any milk or butter with plant-based versions (many boxed mixes call for water, but I always replace that with plant-based milk).

---

1. Preheat the oven to 350°F. Grease an 8 x 8-inch baking pan with the butter or oil.

FOR A HOMEMADE CAKE:

2. In a medium bowl, combine the sugar, milk, melted butter or oil, applesauce, vinegar, and vanilla in a medium bowl and mix well.

3. In a large bowl, whisk together the flour, baking soda, and salt. Pour the wet ingredients into the dry and whisk until smooth. Pour the batter into the prepared pan, smooth the top with a spatula, and bake for 25 to 28 minutes, until a toothpick inserted in the middle comes out clean. Set aside to cool for 2 hours.

FOR A CAKE MIX:

4. Follow the instructions on the cake mix box to make the batter, substituting plant-based ingredients as necessary and adding the vinegar.

(Continued)

(Continued)

THREE "MILKS":

1 cup soy milk

1 cup oat milk, preferably full-fat

1 cup Lechera (page 203) or canned vegan condensed milk

TO SERVE:

Plant-based whipped cream

Fresh strawberries, sliced

5. Pour the batter into the prepared pan, smooth the top with a spatula, and bake according to the box instructions. You can check for doneness by inserting a toothpick in the middle—it should come out clean. Set aside to cool for 2 hours.

TO ASSEMBLE:

6. For the tres leches mixture, in a medium bowl, whisk together the soy milk, oat milk, and lechera until well incorporated.

7. Once the cake has cooled, pierce the cake in multiple places with a fork, then pour about one-third of the milk mixture over the cake. Wait a minute for the cake to soak up the milk, then pour over another third of the liquid. Wait another minute, then pour over the rest. Cover with plastic wrap and refrigerate for at least 2 hours.

8. When ready to serve, cut into squares and top each serving with a layer of whipped cream and fresh strawberries. Store leftovers in a covered container in the fridge for up to 4 days.

CHURROS

MAKES 8 CHURROS

½ cup cane sugar

1½ teaspoons ground cinnamon

DOUGH:

1 cup water

3 tablespoons plus 1 quart neutral high-heat oil, such as avocado oil

2 tablespoons cane sugar

1 teaspoon vanilla extract

¾ teaspoon sea salt

1 cup all-purpose flour

TO SERVE:

Champurrado (page 234)

Cajeta (page 202)

Lechera (page 203) or store-bought vegan condensed milk

Churros are a treat my husband and I indulge in nearly every night during our trips to Mexico City—these fried dough batons with a golden crisp exterior and a soft, slightly chewy, buttery inside, coated with cinnamon sugar, are well worth the visit alone. There is a famous churrería (churro shop) chain in Mexico City called El Moro that cannot be missed. In 1935 they began serving fresh, hot churros that happened to be vegan, as their recipe consists only of flour, water, and salt, fried in oil.

While many credit the Spanish for the introduction of churros to the world, it has been said that the inspiration came originally from a Chinese pastry called youtiao. Wherever the credit lies, it ultimately became a staple dessert, snack, or even breakfast in Mexico, often served with a mug of chocolate caliente (hot chocolate) or Champurrado (page 234) and enjoyed with dipping sauces like melted chocolate or Cajeta (page 202).

---

1. In a shallow bowl, stir together the sugar and cinnamon and set aside.

2. In a medium saucepan, combine the water, 3 tablespoons oil, sugar, vanilla, and salt. Bring to a boil, then remove the pan from the heat and immediately begin stirring in the flour with a heat-resistant spatula or wooden spoon until a dough forms. Let the dough cool until it can be handled, about 15 minutes.

3. Transfer the dough to a piping bag fitted with a 9FT tip or to a churro press.

4. Heat the remaining 1 quart oil in a large pot over medium heat until it reaches 375°F. If you don't have a thermometer, drop a small amount of dough into the oil to test—it should brown in 2 to 3 minutes. Adjust the heat as necessary.

5. Carefully pipe the dough into the oil in 5- to 6-inch-long pieces, cutting the ends with kitchen scissors or a butter knife. Working in batches of 4 or 5 churros at a time, fry for 2 to 3 minutes on each side, until golden, flipping them with kitchen tongs or a fork. Use tongs to transfer each churro to a paper towel–lined plate, then immediately roll them in the cinnamon sugar, making sure they get nice and coated.

6. Serve warm, with a cup of hot champurrado and bowls of cajeta or lechera for dipping.

PAN DE MUERTO

Day of the Dead Sweet Bread

MAKES 4 BREADS

1 cup plain, unsweetened plant-based milk

8 tablespoons cane sugar, divided, plus more for sprinkling

1 (¼-ounce) packet active dry yeast (2¼ teaspoons)

½ cup applesauce

1 tablespoon orange blossom water

Grated zest of 1 orange (about 1 tablespoon)

9 tablespoons melted vegan butter, divided

1 teaspoon sea salt

3 cups all-purpose flour, divided, plus more for dusting

Pan de muerto is a fluffy, soft, sweet bread with a touch of orange blossom flavor and a sugar coating. This pastry fills the homes of Mexican families from October into early November for the celebration of Día de Muertos (Day of the Dead, called Mikailwitl and Wey Mikailwitl in Indigenous Mesoamerican tradition), to honor ancestors and relatives who have passed on. Beyond the deliciousness of this unique sweet bread, there is a symbolic meaning to every element of the pastry. The round shape of the bread represents the circle of life and death. The ball in the center symbolizes the skull of the deceased, and the pieces that lie across the bread represent the bones of the dead. Pan de muerto is typically placed on ofrendas (altars) as a symbolic offering. Every year, my family and I embrace Día de Muertos as a beautiful way to remember our loved ones who we miss dearly. The moment I smell the delicious scent of pan de muerto in the air as I walk through my local Mexican grocery store, I run home, take out all my baking ingredients, light a candle, play music that reminds me of my grandparents, and make my vegan version with the intention and care that this recipe and my ancestors deserve. I let my mind wander as I remember all the deeply cherished memories made with my angel relatives. *Note: Orange blossom water can be found in Mexican and Middle Eastern grocery stores and online.*

---

1. In a small heatproof bowl, microwave the milk for 1 minute, until the mixture is warm to the touch but not hot. (Alternatively, heat the milk in a small saucepan over low heat.)

2. Transfer the milk to a large bowl, add 2 tablespoons cane sugar and the yeast, and mix well. Set aside for 10 minutes; the yeast should be foaming.

3. Add the applesauce, orange blossom water, orange zest, remaining 6 tablespoons sugar, 6 tablespoons melted butter, and salt and mix well with a spoon. Add 2 cups flour and whisk until the flour is completely incorporated. Add the remaining 1 cup flour and, using a wooden spoon, mix until combined.

4. Dust a work surface generously with flour. Place the dough on the floured surface and knead for 6 minutes, or until the dough is soft and smooth.

5. Wash and dry the large bowl, then grease with 1 tablespoon melted butter. Add the dough to the bowl, cover with a kitchen towel or plastic wrap, and let sit in a warm, dark place for 1 hour; the dough should roughly double in size.

6. Remove the towel and punch down the dough. Divide the dough into 5 even dome-shaped balls and cover with plastic wrap. Let sit for 10 minutes.

7. Preheat the oven to 350°F. Line a rimmed baking sheet with parchment paper.

8. Divide one dough ball into 4 even pieces to create skull and bone flourishes for each of the four breads. For each bread's flourishes, take the divided dough ball and split into 5 even pieces. Roll 1 piece into a small ball (the skull) and the remaining 4 into 3-inch logs (the bones). Using your index fingers, create 2 indentations near the ends of each log, so they somewhat resemble a bone. Repeat with remaining 3 pieces of dough.

9. Place the remaining 4 domed dough balls on the prepared baking sheet. On each one, lay 4 "bones" across one another, then place the small dough ball in the center. Cover with plastic wrap and let sit for 20 minutes; the breads will puff up slightly.

10. Brush the breads with 1 tablespoon melted butter. Bake for 20 to 25 minutes, until golden brown on top.

11. Allow the breads to cool for 30 to 40 minutes. Brush with the remaining 1 tablespoon melted butter and immediately cover generously with cane sugar.

ARROZ CON LECHE

Mexican Rice Pudding

SERVES 6

3 cups water

2 cinnamon sticks

Peel of 1 small orange

½ teaspoon sea salt

1 cup long-grain white rice

3 cups plain, unsweetened plant-based milk

1 cup Lechera (page 203) or canned store-bought vegan condensed milk

Cane sugar (optional)

Raisins (optional)

Medjool dates (optional), chopped

My first memories of arroz con leche—a creamy cinnamon rice porridge with a hint of orange peel—are in my Abuelita Eva's kitchen. She would always make a large pot of this rich, velvety dessert, enough for everyone to take some home. It tasted even better in the following days, straight from the fridge, and that has always been my favorite way to enjoy it, although many like it warm as well. This dessert is beloved not only in Mexican homes, but across all of Latin America. To make a decadent vegan version come to life, I simply swap in plant-based milk; I particularly love oat milk as I find it to be the creamiest. I also use homemade lechera, although a store-bought vegan condensed milk can be substituted. Lastly, raisins are a completely optional addition, as I know they're divisive—you either love them or hate them! If you find yourself in the latter camp, chopped dates can also be a great option and, although not traditionally used, they add a great sweetness and texture to the dish. Add them when serving.

---

1. Combine the water, cinnamon sticks, orange peel, and salt in a large pot. Bring to a boil over high heat and boil for 15 minutes.
2. Meanwhile, put the rice in a fine-mesh strainer and rinse under cool running water for 30 seconds.
3. After 15 minutes, add the rice to the pot and bring to a simmer. Cover, turn the heat down to low, and cook for 17 to 20 minutes, until the rice is fully cooked. You should still see a bit of water in the pot at this point.
4. While the rice cooks, in a small pot, bring the milk to a low simmer. Add the lechera, mix well, and remove the pot from the heat.
5. Once the rice is cooked, remove the cinnamon sticks and orange peel. Add the milk mixture to the rice and cook over low heat for 20 minutes, stirring frequently.
6. Taste and adjust the sweetness. For me, the condensed milk makes it perfectly sweet, but feel free to add sugar to your liking. Enjoy hot or cold. Store in a covered container in the fridge for up to 5 days.

BEBIDAS

Drinks

with and without alcohol

CHAMANGO

Frozen Chamoy Mango Smoothie

SERVES 2

1 cup frozen mango chunks

1½ cups coconut water

Juice of 1 lime

Small handful ice

Chamoy (page 55), for the rim (optional)

Tajín Seasoning, for the rim (optional)

½ cup store-bought chamoy (such as Tajín or Mega)

1 mango, peeled, pitted, and cubed

Growing up just fifteen minutes from the Mexican border meant that my community was heavily influenced by Mexican culture through food. My neighborhood had several fruterías, or Mexican juice bars that serve smoothies, juices, and antojitos. One of these antojitos is chamango, a frozen mango beverage that has layers of fresh mango chunks, chili powder, and chamoy, a tangy, sweet, and sometimes spicy sauce. The sweetness of mango pairs so well with the tang and spice of chamoy, and the duo also make up a common roadside snack in Mexico, with the sauce drizzled on "mango lollipops" (chunks of the fruit speared on sticks). It was a lucky day when my parents would treat my siblings and me to a trip to the frutería for a chamango. While this drink is incredibly enjoyable as is, it is also great spiked with a shot or two of tequila—simply blend it into the beverage with the mango, coconut water, lime juice, and ice! We use two different types of chamoy here since the homemade version is much thicker and thus better for garnishing.

---

1. Combine the frozen mango, coconut water, lime juice, and ice in a blender and blend on high until smooth.

2. If you wish to rim your glass, spoon a bit of homemade chamoy on a small plate and sprinkle some Tajín on another small plate. Press the rim of each glass into the chamoy, then dip it into the Tajín; it's up to you whether you'd like the whole rim coated (in which case you can rotate the glass to fully cover the rim with both garnishes) or just a small portion (in which case you can just dip and lift the glass without rotating).

3. Fill each glass halfway with the frozen mango mixture, then drizzle some of the store-bought chamoy across the top. Add fresh mango cubes, fill each glass with more of the frozen mixture, and garnish with more chamoy and fresh mango.

AGUA DE TAMARINDO Y DÁTIL

Tamarind-Date Agua Fresca

Aguas frescas were created in the pre-Columbian era when the Aztec people mashed and ground fruits, seeds, and flowers into water to create refreshing beverages. Today one of the most popular flavors is agua de tamarindo (tamarind). Tamarind is a tropical fruit with a tough shell and a sticky, soft fruit inside that tastes both sweet and sour. It was introduced to Mexico by the Spanish in the 16th century and is now a staple in Mexican candies and Ponche Navideño (page 249). Aguas frescas are traditionally sweetened with lots of white sugar, but I really love taking the processed sugar content down by substituting dates for natural sweetness. The dates add a honey-like flavor and have natural caramel-like notes that play really nicely with the tamarind!

SERVES 10

10 tamarind pods (about 1 pound), shelled

8 Medjool dates, pitted

8 cups water, divided

½ cup cane sugar

Ice

1. Put the tamarind pods and dates in a large bowl and cover with 6 cups very hot water. Let soak for 1 hour. Once cooled, use your hands to squeeze out the seeds from the softened tamarind pods and discard. Transfer the water, tamarind pulp, and dates to a blender and blend on high for 2 minutes, or until smooth.

2. Hold a fine-mesh strainer over a large pitcher and pour the liquid through. Use a spoon to help the liquid through the strainer. Discard the pulp in the strainer. Add 2 cups fresh water and cane sugar. Using a long wooden spoon, mix well to combine. Taste and add more sugar if desired. Serve over ice.

AGUA DE COCO Y NUEZ

Coconut-Pecan Agua Fresca

SERVES 8

1 cup pecans

5 Medjool dates, pitted

1 cinnamon stick

½ to ¾ cup shredded unsweetened coconut

8 cups water

1 cup brown sugar

1 teaspoon vanilla extract

¼ teaspoon sea salt

Ice

Agua fresca is a Mexican staple crafted for cool refreshment on hot days. It's usually a mixture of fruit juices and water with a little sweetener, but it can really be made of any ingredients soaked or blended into a chilled drink. Another favorite refreshing treat is the raspado, a Mexican take on a snow cone: shaved ice with different syrups from tropical fruit to tamarind and even nut-based ones like pecan. I have many childhood memories of crossing the border to Tijuana for the day with my longtime best friend Alexis and her family to indulge in tacos and raspados. I would always order coco (coconut) and nuez (pecan) flavor. When I am missing the days of joyfully enjoying raspados as a child, I make this sweet, rich, creamy beverage, which is that same combo but in liquid form, poured over ice. This decadent drink is such a lovely treat to enjoy on a weekend and even delicious as an iced latte: my husband, Chancy, loves adding a double shot of espresso to his agua de coco y nuez.

1. Combine the pecans, dates, cinnamon stick, and ½ cup shredded coconut in a medium bowl and cover with water. Let soak for 2 hours or overnight. Drain. Transfer the ingredients to a blender, along with the fresh water, brown sugar, vanilla, and salt. Blend on high for 1 to 2 minutes, until smooth. Place a nut milk bag or cheesecloth over a large bowl or pitcher and pour the mixture through. Discard the contents of the bag.

2. If you would like to add some texture, return the liquid to the blender, along with another ¼ cup shredded coconut, and pulse 3 or 4 times. Do not strain.

3. Pour over ice and enjoy! Store leftovers in a covered container in the fridge for up to 4 days.

AGUA DE PIÑA Y JAMAICA

Pineapple-Hibiscus Agua Fresca

SERVES 6

1 cup dried hibiscus flowers

4 cups water, divided

¼ cup cane sugar

2 cups fresh pineapple chunks

Ice

Agua de jamaica is what I like to call my happy drink. Dried hibiscus flowers have incredible health properties, and studies have shown them to be a natural antidepressant. When I am having a difficult mental health week, I often make a large batch of agua de jamaica to have throughout the week. This refreshingly tart yet sweet drink is so enjoyable and always serves as a mood booster, and in this recipe, the addition of pineapple adds a lovely tropical sweetness. I also sometimes add a cinnamon stick. It's fun to get creative and add a new layer of flavor to a drink that is already so tasty on its own, and this adaptability and resourcefulness is one of my favorite facets of Mexican cooking.

---

1. Combine the hibiscus flowers and 2 cups water in a medium pot and bring to a soft boil over medium heat. Remove the pan from the heat, stir in the sugar, and set aside to cool.

2. Meanwhile, combine the pineapple and remaining 2 cups water in a blender, reserving 6 pieces of pineapple for garnish. Blend on high for 1 minute. Let sit for 10 minutes.

3. Hold a fine-mesh strainer over a pitcher and carefully pour the cooled hibiscus water into a pitcher. (Reserve the hibiscus flowers for Taquitos de Flor de Jamaica, page 152.) For a smooth drink, pour the blended pineapple through the strainer; for a more textured drink, pour the contents of the blender directly into the pitcher, including the pineapple pulp.

4. Mix well, then taste and add more sugar if desired. Pour over ice and garnish with a piece of pineapple.

✻ JUGO VERDE DE ABUELO ✻

Grandpa's Green Juice

SERVES 2

Jugo verde has always been *it* in Mexican culture. No matter where you go in Mexico, you should be able to find fresh juices being made on the streets or in mercados, and this one is a perennial favorite. My Grandpa Alfonso made a jugo every morning and would remind me of it every time I saw him. He would proudly tell me, "Mijita, yo hago mi jugo verde diario," and would proceed to tell me all the latest fruits and vegetables he had added to his jugo. This recipe is one of those many iterations I am honored to share. I love to play the song "Volver, Volver" by Vicente Fernandez while I make this recipe, because it truly embodies my grandfather in every way.

---

1 cup fresh pineapple chunks

½ cup spinach

¼ cup chopped, peeled fresh aloe

½ green apple, cored

2 celery ribs

½ cucumber

½ cup water

Ice (optional)

Combine all the ingredients in a blender and blend on high for 45 seconds, or until smooth. Hold a fine-mesh strainer over a glass and pour in the blended mixture. (Alternatively, juice all the ingredients in a juicer, omitting the water.) Enjoy with or without ice.

CAFÉ DE OLLA

Traditional Mexican Coffee

The scent of coffee made in an olla de barro (traditional Mexican ceramic pot) with warm spices, sweetened with piloncillo, is the most divine smell to have radiating throughout your home on a weekend morning. When you arrive at a traditional restaurant in Mexico for breakfast, you're often immediately offered a cup of café de olla, and it's something I can't ever turn down. It is a unique experience, as it truly warms the body from head to toe with its spices and a natural caramel-like sweetness.

While the coffee can be made in a normal pot, a traditional olla de barro makes for an authentic experience, as many say there is a difference in taste when the coffee is prepared in its most traditional way.

SERVES 6

3 cardamom pods

8 cups water

1 (4-ounce) piece piloncillo

1 cinnamon stick

4 whole cloves

½ cup ground coffee

Plain, unsweetened plant-based milk (optional)

---

1. Put the cardamom pods in a molcajete or mortar and crush the pods to expose the seeds inside.

2. In a large pot or cured olla de barro (see page 20), combine the water, piloncillo, cinnamon stick, cloves, and mashed cardamom. Bring to a soft boil over medium heat and boil for 25 minutes, then add the coffee and stir. Remove the pot from the heat and let the coffee steep for 15 minutes.

3. Hold a fine-mesh strainer over a jar or large bowl and pour in the contents of the pot; discard the solids in the strainer. Return the coffee to the pot and simmer over medium heat for 5 minutes.

4. Pour the coffee into mugs. Enjoy the traditional way, black, or with a splash of milk.

CHOCOLATE FRÍO

Mexican Iced Hot Chocolate

SERVES 2

1 cup water

1 small cinnamon stick, broken into 2 or 3 pieces

1½ cups plain, unsweetened plant-based milk

⅓ (3.3.-ounce) Mexican chocolate disk (such as Ibarra), roughly chopped

½ ounce dark chocolate, plus more for garnish

¼ teaspoon vanilla extract

Sea salt

Ice

Memories of sitting in a café in Oaxaca, sipping on a chocolate frío, will always stay with me. It is one of those very simple but very special experiences that have been imprinted in my mind forever. I long for those moments of sitting in a lively, airy cafe and being able to order a chocolate caliente o frío (hot or cold) made with high-quality cacao. While most Mexican cacao is grown in Oaxaca's neighboring states Chiapas and Tabasco, some cacao is also grown in Oaxaca, making the memory that much more special. The tradition of enjoying a frothy cacao beverage came from the Indigenous people of Mesoamerica, where it served as a spiritual and ceremonious symbol. Every Indigenous community prepared their cacao differently, depending on what ingredients were available to them, some including chiles or spices and others adding maíz (maize), creating something we know as Champurrado (page 234). My rendition of this delicious ancient beverage has a touch of cinnamon. Make this drink in the morning for a boost of energy or in the evening for a tasty after-dinner treat.

---

1. In a medium pot, combine the water and cinnamon pieces. Bring to a simmer over medium heat. Add the milk, both chocolates, the vanilla, and a small pinch of salt. Bring to a simmer, whisking so that the chocolates melt. Remove the pot from the heat and set aside for 15 to 20 minutes to cool.

2. Pour the chocolate mixture into a cocktail shaker, add a handful of ice, and shake for 10 to 15 seconds. Put fresh ice in each glass. Hold a fine-mesh strainer over each glass and pour in the chocolate mixture. Garnish with shaved chocolate on top.

CHAMPURRADO

Extra Creamy Mexican Hot Chocolate

SERVES 6

Champurrado is the creamiest hot chocolate, with an extra layer of richness that cannot be found in a typical hot chocolate. A beverage that is typically reserved for the coziest of moments like Christmas or Día de Muertos, champurrado is a chocolate version of atole, a warm masa-based beverage with indigenous roots. This traditional hot chocolate is uniquely thickened with masa harina to create the most luscious, satisfying cup of comfort with hints of nuttiness and earthiness from the addition of maíz (maize). Enjoy with Conchas (page 210) or Pan de Muerto (page 218) for the ultimate Mexican indulgence.

3½ cups water, divided

1 cinnamon stick

4 whole cloves

1 (4-ounce) piece piloncillo

3 cups plain, unsweetened plant-based milk

1½ (3.3-ounce) disks Mexican chocolate (such as Ibarra), roughly chopped

½ cup masa harina (instant/nixtamalized corn masa flour)

1. In a large pot, bring 2 cups water, the cinnamon stick, cloves, and piloncillo to a simmer over medium heat. Add the milk and chocolate and simmer for 7 minutes, whisking so that the chocolate melts.

2. Meanwhile, combine the masa harina and remaining 1½ cups water in a blender and blend on high for 1 minute.

3. Hold a large strainer over the pot and pour the masa mixture through it. Mix to combine, turn the heat down to low, and simmer for 10 minutes. Whisk well, then taste and adjust the sweetness to your liking. Pour into mugs and enjoy.

HORCHATA CHOCOLATE

SERVES 6

1 cup uncooked long-grain white rice

9 cups water, divided

1 large or 2 small cinnamon sticks, plus more for garnish

1 cup raw unsalted cashews

¼ cup plus 2 tablespoons cocoa powder, plus more for dusting

½ cup cane sugar

¼ teaspoon sea salt

Ice

I adore horchata (Mexican rice milk). I also adore chocolate with every fiber of my being—dramatic, I know, but it's true. This chocolate horchata is a dream: it's silky smooth, slightly sweet, and the perfect drink to enjoy with friends and family after a meal or as a midday pick-me-up. *Note: You will need a nut milk bag or cheesecloth.*

---

1. Put the rice in a blender and pulse 10 times to break it down. (It does not have to be a powder, just smaller pieces.)
2. Add 3 cups water to the blender, along with the cinnamon stick and cashews, and let everything soak in the blender for 4 hours or overnight. Drain in a colander in the sink, then return the strained ingredients to the blender, along with the remaining 6 cups water. Blend on high for 2 minutes.
3. Place a nut milk bag or cheesecloth over a large bowl or pitcher and pour the mixture through. Discard the contents of the bag. Return the liquid to the blender, add the cocoa powder, sugar, and salt, and blend on high for 1 minute.
4. Pour over ice, garnish with a cinnamon stick, and dust with cocoa powder.

CÓCTEL DE CAFÉ

Mexican White Russian

MAKES 2 COCKTAILS

CAFÉ DE OLLA CONCENTRATE:

1½ cups water

1 cinnamon stick

2 whole cloves

1 (2-inch) piece piloncillo *or* ¼ cup brown sugar

Heaping ¼ cup ground coffee

COCKTAIL:

Agave syrup, for the rim

Brown sugar, for the rim

3 ounces tequila blanco

Ice

4 ounces oat milk

2 cinnamon sticks and/or a few whole coffee beans

This spiced, creamy cocktail is my husband's creation, a Mexican version of a white Russian. This cocktail replaced an obsession with espresso martinis for my friends after my sweet husband, Chancy, was experimenting and served this up to us. He has a deep appreciation and love for both coffee and mixology, so it was only a matter of time before he combined the two and this divine, genius drink was born. As my friends and I all went around the table recapping our weeks, joyfully sipping this smooth cóctel, we realized that we'd discovered our new favorite nightcap. And for those who prefer a caffeine-free version, simply use decaf coffee. *Note: The concentrate makes enough for 4 cocktails, but an average shaker will provide room for only 2, so either make 2 rounds of cocktails or store the extra concentrate in a covered container in the fridge for up to 1 week (it can also be used in a latte or iced coffee).*

---

1. To make the concentrate, in a medium pot, combine the water, cinnamon stick, cloves, and piloncillo and bring to a boil over medium-high heat. Boil for 15 minutes, then add the ground coffee and remove the pot from the heat. Set aside until completely cool, 30 to 45 minutes. Hold a fine-mesh strainer over a jar and pour the coffee mixture through it; discard the solids in the strainer.

2. To rim the cocktail glasses, put a bit of agave on a small plate and a bit of brown sugar on another small plate. Press the rim of each glass into the agave, then dip into the brown sugar; it's up to you whether you'd like the whole rim coated (in which case you can rotate the glass to fully cover the rim with both garnishes) or just a small portion (in which case you can just dip and lift the glass without rotating).

3. In a cocktail shaker, combine 4 ounces of the café de olla concentrate, the tequila, and a handful of ice, then secure the lid and shake 8 to 10 times.

4. Put fresh ice in each glass. Hold a fine-mesh strainer over each glass and fill three-quarters of the way with the cocktail, then fill the rest of each glass with milk. Garnish with a cinnamon stick and/or whole coffee beans and enjoy!

PALOMA FRESCA

MAKES 2 COCKTAILS

Citrusy, tart, bubbly, and refreshing, the national drink of Mexico, the paloma, is simple yet delightful. It's usually made from a combination of tequila, lime juice, and a grapefruit-flavored soda, typically Squirt, Fresca, or Jarritos. While using soda is traditional, I couldn't help but wonder how delicious the combination of fresh grapefruit juice and sparkling water would be. One taste of my husband Chancy's fresh juice version was enough for us to be hooked and forget the soda version ever existed!

---

4 ounces tequila blanco

6 ounces fresh grapefruit juice, plus 2 grapefruit wedges for garnish

1 ounce fresh lime juice

1½ ounces simple syrup

Ice

Sparkling water (such as Topo Chico)

1. In a cocktail shaker, combine the tequila, grapefruit juice, lime juice, simple syrup, and a handful of ice, secure the lid, and shake for 15 to 20 seconds.

2. Put fresh ice in the cocktail glasses. Hold a fine-mesh strainer over each glass and pour in the cocktail, stopping ½ inch from the rim. Top off with a splash of sparkling water. Garnish with a thinly sliced grapefruit wedge.

MARGARITA DE JALAPEÑO

Spicy Jalapeño Margarita

You can never go wrong with a spicy margarita. If you walk into my parents' home for any occasion, you will hear salsa music and my dad will immediately offer to make you a margarita...truly an exceptional home to walk into! So put on some Marc Anthony music and enjoy the perfect margarita. Serve alongside Tacos de "Chicharrón" de Setas en Salsa Verde (page 149) for a most delicious pairing. *Note: If you want a classic margarita without the spice, simply ditch the jalapeño.*

MAKES 2 COCKTAILS

Chamoy (page 55), for the rim

Tajín Seasoning, for the rim

½ jalapeño pepper, cut into ¼-inch slices

4 ounces tequila blanco

3 ounces triple sec

3 ounces fresh lemon juice (from about 2 lemons)

2 ounces fresh lime juice (from about 2 limes)

2 ounces simple syrup

Ice

1. To rim the cocktail glasses, spoon a bit of chamoy on a small plate and sprinkle some Tajín on another plate. Dip the rim of each glass into the chamoy, then into the Tajín; it's up to you whether you'd like the whole rim coated (in which case you can rotate the glass to fully cover the rim with both garnishes) or just a small portion (in which case you can just dip and lift the glass without rotating).

2. Put the jalapeño slices in a cocktail shaker, reserving 2 slices for garnish, and, using a cocktail muddler or the handle of a wooden spoon, muddle well. Add the tequila, triple sec, lemon juice, lime juice, simple syrup, and a handful of ice, then secure the lid and shake for 15 to 20 seconds.

3. Put fresh ice in each glass. Hold a fine-mesh strainer over each glass and pour in the cocktail. Top with a fresh slice of jalapeño and enjoy.

MARGARITA DE MANGO

Mango Margarita

MAKES 2 COCKTAILS

- Sea salt or Tajín Seasoning, for the rim
- Lime wedge, for the rim
- ½ mango, peeled and diced, or ¼ cup frozen mango chunks, thawed
- 4 ounces tequila blanco
- 4 ounces mango juice
- 2 ounces fresh lime juice (from about 2 limes)
- 2 ounces simple syrup
- Ice

The deepest yellow-orange mango margarita was placed in front of me while I was out to dinner one night at a restaurant in Mexico City called Azul. I could see just how good it would taste by the fresh mango pulp floating around in the glass. Just one sip of the cocktail and I looked over at my husband, Chancy, and asked if he could make it at home as soon as mango season rolls in, which for us in California is summer. A mango is ripe, juicy, and sweetest when it is soft to the touch, with a similar feel to a ripe peach and a sweet, ripe scent. This drink can also be made with frozen mango, for those times when you're missing the flavors of summer.

---

1. To rim the cocktail glasses, sprinkle a bit of salt or Tajín on a small plate. Rub the rim of each glass with the lime wedge, then dip the rim into the salt or Tajín.
2. Put the mango in a shaker and, using a cocktail muddler or the handle of a wooden spoon, muddle well. Add the tequila, mango juice, lime juice, simple syrup, and a handful of ice, then secure the lid and shake for 15 to 20 seconds.
3. Put fresh ice in each glass. Hold a fine-mesh strainer over each glass and pour in the cocktail.

MARGARITA DE PEPINO

Cucumber Margarita

MAKES 2 COCKTAILS

Tajín Seasoning, for the rim

Lime wedge, for the rim

1 large cucumber

¼ cup water

4 ounces tequila blanco

2 ounces triple sec

2 ounces lime juice

2 ounces simple syrup or agave syrup

Ice

A fresh, bright, light drink that will make you want to lie out on a beach and soak up the sun, this margarita was inspired by agua de pepino, one of our favorite aguas frescas for its refreshing and tart citrusy flavor, and one that I make frequently because there is always a cucumber in our fridge that needs to be used up! Serve these delicious margaritas with Ceviche de Palmito (page 109) for a fresh summer menu.

---

1. To rim the cocktail glasses, sprinkle a bit of Tajín on a small plate. Rub the rim of each glass with the lime wedge, then dip the rim into the Tajín.

2. Cut one-eighth of the cucumber into thin rounds and set aside 2 for garnish. Put the remaining rounds in a cocktail shaker and set aside. Cut the rest of the cucumber into 1-inch piece and transfer to a blender, along with the water. Blend on high for 45 seconds, or until smooth.

3. Using a cocktail muddler or the handle of a wooden spoon, muddle the cucumber in the cocktail shaker. Add 4 ounces of the blended cucumber juice, the tequila, triple sec, lime juice, simple syrup, and a handful of ice, secure the lid, and shake for 15 to 20 seconds.

4. Put fresh ice in each glass. Hold a fine-mesh strainer over each glass and pour in the cocktail. Top with the reserved cucumber slices and enjoy!

MEZCALITA DE PIÑA

Pineapple Mezcal Margarita

MAKES 2 COCKTAILS

Sea salt or Tajín Seasoning, for the rim

Lime wedge, for the rim

¼ fresh pineapple, peeled, cored, and cut into 1-inch-thick disks

3 ounces mezcal

5 ounces pineapple juice (such as Dole)

1½ ounces simple syrup

½ ounce fresh lime juice

Ice

Mezcal and pineapple are a match made in heaven. Mezcal is similar to tequila in that it is an alcohol derived from the agave plant. To make mezcal, the agave goes through an artisanal process. It is roasted underground with coals, then insulated for a long and slow roasting process, creating a smoky, slightly sweet alcoholic sprit. While you can certainly use fresh pineapple in this cocktail, grilling or roasting the fruit brings out a caramelized sweetness that is incredible when muddled into a cocktail, and so worth the extra effort. I especially love to pair this smoky and sweet margarita with Gringa al Pastor Tacos (page 141), as it is the ideal way to use up a whole pineapple and enjoy the beloved duo of tacos and margaritas.

---

1. To rim the cocktail glasses, sprinkle a bit of salt or Tajín on a small plate. Rub the rim of each glass with the lime wedge, then dip the rim into the salt or Tajín.
2. On an outdoor grill or stovetop grill pan over medium-high heat, grill the pineapple disks for 1 to 2 minute on each side, until grill marks appear. Transfer to a cutting board and roughly chop into small chunks.
3. Put the grilled pineapple chunks in a cocktail shaker, reserving 2 pieces for garnish, and, using a cocktail muddler or the handle of a wooden spoon, muddle well. Add the mezcal, pineapple juice, simple syrup, lime juice, and a handful of ice, then secure the lid and shake for 15 to 20 seconds.
4. Put fresh ice in each glass. Hold a fine-mesh strainer over each glass and pour in the cocktail. Garnish with a piece of grilled pineapple and enjoy!

MEZCALITA DE JAMAICA Y FRESA

Hibiscus and Strawberry Mezcal Margarita

MAKES 2 COCKTAILS

¼ cup dried hibiscus flowers

¾ cup water

Cane sugar, for the rim

Lime wedge, for the rim

1-inch piece orange peel

2 strawberries, hulled and sliced

4 ounces mezcal

1½ ounces simple syrup

1 ounce fresh lime juice

1 ounce fresh orange juice

Ice

I traveled to the beautiful city of Oaxaca with my family for the first time a few years ago. We were welcomed with shots of mezcal. Coming from a family of tequila lovers, I bravely and graciously drank it up and was quickly surprised by how different and unique the flavor was, as it hit the back of my throat with big smoky notes. I was not too sure I would want to drink this spirit again, until I found myself sitting on a rooftop balcony in the center of Oaxaca and saw a flor de jamaica and strawberry mezcal margarita on the menu. I was so impressed with how well the jamaica married into the flavor of mezcal and delighted by the subtly sweet background flavor of orange and strawberry. After our trip, my then-fiancé, Chancy, excitedly recreated this cocktail at home and we loved it so much, we added it to the drink menu at our wedding!

---

1. Combine the hibiscus flowers and water in a small pot. Bring to a simmer over medium heat and simmer for 4 minutes, then remove the pan from the heat and let sit for at least 15 minutes to steep and cool.

2. To rim the cocktail glasses, sprinkle a bit of cane sugar on a small plate. Rub the rim of each glass with the lime wedge, then dip the rim into the sugar.

3. Put the orange peel and strawberries in a cocktail shaker, reserving 2 strawberry slices for garnish, and, using a cocktail muddler or the handle of a wooden spoon, muddle well. Add the mezcal, simple syrup, lime juice, orange juice, hibiscus mixture, and a handful of ice, secure the lid, and shake for 15 to 20 seconds.

4. Put fresh ice in each glass. Hold a fine-mesh strainer over each glass and pour in the cocktail. Top with a fresh strawberry slice.

PONCHE NAVIDEÑO

Mexican Christmas Punch

SERVES 10

12 cups water

2 large tamarind pods, shelled

¼ cup dried hibiscus flowers

1 cinnamon stick

8 Mexican hawthorn (optional)

5 guavas, diced

1 orange, peeled and diced

1 green apple, cored and diced

6 pieces sugarcane (optional)

¼ cup cane sugar

This cozy, fruity, spiced, warming drink is enjoyed at Christmastime, specifically on Nochebuena (Christmas Eve). It tastes like the holidays in a cup or like a warm, loving hug from your grandmother. Every family has their own rendition of ponche navideño, and this is one I adapted from my own family's recipe. The recipe includes unique yet traditional ingredients for ponche, like tejocote (Mexican hawthorn). It looks like a mini apple, with a sweet and sour flavor similar to apricot. These little gems can be found in Mexican markets around the holidays. Another special ingredient to search for in your local Mexican market is tamarind, which can be found in its natural shell. I invite you to adjust the recipe to your liking and use what is available to you; sub in apricots or plums for the hawthorn, add anise, adjust the sweetness, and get creative with different warming spices and fruits!

---

1. In a large pot, combine the water, tamarind, hibiscus, and cinnamon stick. Bring to a boil over medium heat and boil for 10 minutes. Add the hawthorn (if using), guavas, orange, apple, sugarcane (if using), and sugar, cover, and boil for 15 to 20 minutes.

2. Taste and add more sugar to your liking. Ladle the hot ponche into mugs, adding as much fruit to each serving as you'd like.

ACKNOWLEDGMENTS

Chancy James, thank you for being my absolute rock throughout this entire process, for physically and emotionally being there through every single step of the way. You encouraged me when I most needed it and have always been my biggest hype man. Lastly, thank you for creating the most delicious cocktails for this book and being my personal bartender for life!

To my parents, for giving me a life so full of love, family, and cultura. I am who I am because of the beautiful foundation you built. A mi Papá, gracias por apoyarme siempre como nadie. Has sido mi fan número uno desde el primer día. Mamacita, thank you for exemplifying what it is to work hard and go after what I hope and dream for. Los amo muchísimo.

To my angel Tía Esther. Seven years ago I came out with a digital cookbook. You printed the entire digital book and put it in your kitchen as if it was a published cookbook and I remember thinking one day I would make you extra proud with an actual published cookbook. I wish so badly you were here. I know you're proud of me up in heaven.

To my agent, Stacey, thank you for believing in me, understanding and seeing my vision, and helping me reach my dream.

To Thea, my editor, thank you for seeing potential in me to write the book of my dreams, for seeing value in sharing my culture, my family, and my recipes. Thank you for your patience, for pushing me to my fullest potential. I hope after this long journey, I have made you proud.

A gigantic thank you to the incredible team at Hachette Book Group—Julianna Lee, Pat Jalbert-Levine, Nyamekye Waliyaya, Katherine Akey, Lauren Ortiz, Karen Wise, and Suzanne Fass—for all the hard work and many hours put into making *Plantas* come to life. I am incredibly grateful, as it wouldn't be what it is without all of you!

To Emily, my best friend and the best VA to ever exist, for quite literally keeping me sane and helping my business succeed throughout the entire book journey. Thank you for always reminding me to take care of myself and for being such a solid support throughout the process.

To my Instagram community, you truly feel like family. It's been more than eight years of sharing with you my love for cooking, bits of my life, and my mental health chats and advocacy. I can't thank you enough for being the most kind and supportive community. Thank you from the bottom of my heart for picking up my book and supporting something physical and beyond social media.

To my cookbook author friends, especially Remy Morimoto Park, Andrea Aliseda, and Toni Okamoto, thank you for letting me vent on some of the hardest days in the cookbook journey, for being there to lift me up and encouraging me when I most needed it.

To my sister, Stefania, my very best friend in the world. Our hour-long daily phone calls get me through the toughest, longest days. You help heal in more ways than you know.

To my cousin Jessica Smith, for willingly reading my very rough (literally and figuratively) draft and for giving your valued input and advice. Because of your immense appreciation and love for reading and cookbooks, I hope I have made you proud.

A mi Abuelita Eva en el cielo, siempre serás mi inspiración. Mi amor por la cocina es gracias a ti.

A mi grandma Esther, gracias por dejarme hermosos recuerdos de tu casa, tu cocina, y tu alma, estas en mi corazón por siempre.

To Vanessa, my creative primita. Thank you for helping me create the cover of *Plantas*. I knew you were the one person that I could explain my vision to, and then help me bring it to life!

To my mother-in-law, Ter Bear, for being the first person to truly teach me things in the kitchen ten years ago! Thank you for sharing your love of cooking with me.

A mi Tía Cristy, muchisimas gracias por ser un luz grandísimo en mi vida y por tu tiempo ese fin en donde nos sentamos y buscamos recetas de mi abuelita, Tía Pilla, y de la familia Peña.

A mi Chopis, Sofia, gracias por abrirme tu casita y cocina. Es gracias a tu casita llena de puro amor, que yo pude crear para este libro. Eres la mejor amiga.

To Edgar, for being an incredible guide and friend and being so willing to help me with your incredible expertise as an author, food stylist, and photographer.

To Kedrin, my longtime childhood best friend, from the second I got my first cookbook offer to now, you have cared immensely and supported me throughout the entire process. You're always there and I thank you so much.

A Fon, por ser un amigo tan increíble. Gracias a ti y a tu familia por abrirme tu hermosa casa en Valle para poder esconderme y escribir para el libro.

To my brother, Alec, you don't know this, but on a very stressful cookbook day, you sent me the sweetest, most encouraging message out of the blue. Thank you for being so supportive and loving throughout my entire life.

To my lifelong best friend, Alexis, and my second parents (the Magallaneses). Thank you for believing in me from day one. Your allowing me to use your kitchen for a photo shoot for my digital cookbook seven years ago meant the world to me.

ABOUT THE AUTHOR

Alexa Soto is a Mexican American recipe creator, mental health advocate, and the creator of the blog *Fueled Naturally*. She loves connecting with her audience across social media. She lives in San Diego with her husband, Chancy, their son, Santino, and their two dogs.

INDEX

Note: Page references in *italics* indicate photographs.

Q

R

S